Graphics and Visual Communication for Managers

Robert P. Sedlack, Jr.
Barbara L. Shwom
Karl P. Keller

2 Managerial Communication Series | Editor: James S. O'Rourke, IV

SOUTH-WESTERN
CENGAGE Learning™

Australia • Brazil • Japan • Korea • Mexico • Singapore • Spain • United Kingdom • United States

Graphics and Visual Communication for Managers, Managerial Communication Series

James S. O'Rourke IV, series editor; Robert P. Sedlack, Jr., Barbara L. Shwom, Karl P. Keller

VP/Editorial Director: Jack W. Calhoun

VP/Editor-in-Chief: Melissa Acuña

Acquisitions Editor: Erin Joyner

Developmental Editor: Daniel Noguera

Marketing Manager: Mike Aliscad

Content Project Manager: Jana Lewis

Manager of Technology, Editorial: John Barans

Technology Project Editor: John Rich

Manufacturing Coordinator: Diane Gibbons

Production Service: Pre-Press PMG

Art Director: Stacy Jenkins Shirley

Internal Designer: Robb & Associates

Cover Designer: Robb & Associates

For product information and technology assistance, contact us at
Cengage Learning Academic Resource Center, 1-800-423-0563

For permission to use material from this text or product, submit all requests online at **www.cengage.com/permissions**
Further permissions questions can be emailed to
permissionrequest@cengage.com

Library of Congress Control Number: 2007909664

ISBN-13: 978-0-324-58418-9

ISBN-10: 0-324-58418-0

South-Western Cengage Learning
5191 Natorp Boulevard
Mason, OH 45040
USA

Cengage Learning products are represented in Canada by Nelson Education, Ltd.

For your course and learning solutions, visit **academic.cengage.com**

Purchase any of our products at your local college store or at our preferred online store **www.ichapters.com**

Printed in the United States of America
2 3 4 5 6 7   13 12 11

This is for my family: Pam, Colleen, Jay, Molly, Kathleen.
And, of course, Cianan and our latest addition, Ty.
It's for my colleagues as well: Carolyn, Sandra, Cynthia, and Sondra. Thanks for
all you've done to make my life meaningful, rich, and...busy.
JSO'R IV

To my wife Theresa, for her love, friendship, support, and patience.
To Emma and Trey for reminding me to play.
And to my parents, Bob and Ellen, for the foundation they provided.
RPS Jr.

To all our clients, who keep us grounded in business reality.
And to our son Nat, who keeps us grounded in life.
BLS and KPK

AUTHOR BIOGRAPHIES

James S. O'Rourke teaches management and corporate communication at the University of Notre Dame, where he is Founding Director of the Eugene D. Fanning Center for Business Communication and Concurrent Professor of Management. In a career spanning four decades, he has earned an international reputation in business and corporate communication. *Business Week* magazine has twice named him one of the "outstanding faculty" in Notre Dame's Mendoza College of Business.

His publications include *Management Communication: A Case-Analysis Approach* from Prentice-Hall, now in third edition, and *Business Communication: A Framework for Success* from Thomson South-Western. Professor O'Rourke is also senior editor of an eight-book series on Managerial Communication and is principal author or directing editor of more than 150 management and corporate communication case studies.

Professor O'Rourke is a graduate of Notre Dame with advanced degrees from Temple University, the University of New Mexico, and a PhD in Communication from the S. I. Newhouse School of Syracuse University.

Robert P. Sedlack Jr. is principal of Sedlack Design Associates and is responsible for consultation service, design, and execution of a wide variety of print and multimedia projects to the business and cultural community. His design work has been recognized by *Graphic Design USA*, *Graphis*, *HOW*, and the American Association of Museums.

As a design professor at the University of Notre Dame, Robert's personal research is focused on the life-changing impact that design can have when applied appropriately and collaboratively with organizations dedicated to social betterment. He teaches both undergraduate and graduate design students, and his course work includes projects that tackle various social issues such as discrimination, poverty, and voter participation. Professor Sedlack holds a BFA in Graphic Design from Notre Dame and an MFA in Graphic Design from Indiana University.

Barbara L. Shwom is managing principal of Communication Partners (communipartners.com). For the past 25 years, her commitment to improving communication has informed all aspects of her professional and personal life. As a professor at Northwestern University and the Kellogg School of Management, and as a consultant to business and not-for-profit organizations, she has taught hundreds of students and professionals to be clearer and more strategic about what they say and how they say it.

A nationally recognized leader in business communication, Barbara has served as president of both the Association for Business Communication and the Association of Professional Communication Consultants. Professor Shwom is a graduate of Simmons College and holds a PhD from Northwestern University.

Karl P. Keller, principal of Communication Partners, has held senior executive positions in marketing, strategy, training, and technology in the managed fund, brokerage, venture capital, and private equity industries. He has developed and written business plans and private offerings for capital-raising and revenue growth, has led business teams on developing large-scale technology projects, and has a strong track record in negotiating bottom-line benefits and solving business problems.

Karl is also a dynamic speaker, presenter, and trainer and has created and delivered dozens of seminars across a range of disciplines, including communication, negotiation, accounting, budgeting, investing, and technology. He taught English at Northwestern University and the University of Illinois-Chicago and also worked as a journalist covering real estate development and finance. He is a graduate of Pennsylvania State University and holds an MBA from Northwestern University.

CONTENTS

GRAPHICS AND VISUAL COMMUNICATION FOR MANAGERS

Foreword

In recent years, for a variety of reasons, communication has grown increasingly complex. The issues that seemed so straightforward, so simple, not long ago are now somehow different, more complicated. Has the process changed? Have the elements of communication or the barriers to success been altered? What's different now? Why has this all gotten more difficult?

Several issues are at work here, not the least of which is pacing. Information, images, events, and human activity all move at a much faster pace than they did just a decade ago. Among the more popular, hip new business magazines in recent years is *Fast Company*. Readers are reminded that it's not just a matter of tempo but a new way of living we're experiencing.

Technology has changed things as well. We're now able to communicate with almost anyone, almost anywhere, 24/7 with very little effort and very little professional assistance. It's all possible because of cellular telephone technology, digital imaging, the Internet, fiber optics, global positioning satellites, teleconferencing codecs, high-speed data processing, online data storage and...well, the list goes on and on. What's new this morning will be old hat by lunch.

Culture has intervened in our lives in some important ways. Very few parts of the world are inaccessible anymore. Other people's beliefs, practices, perspectives, and possessions are as familiar to us as our own. And for many of us, we're only now coming to grips with the idea that our own beliefs aren't shared by everyone and that culture is hardly value neutral.

The nature of the world in which we live—one that's wired, connected, mobile, fast-paced, iconically visual, and far less driven by logic—has changed in some not-so-subtle ways in recent days. The organizations that employ us and the businesses that depend on our skills now recognize that communication is at the center of what it means to be successful—and at the heart of what it means to be human.

To operate profitably means that business must now conduct itself in responsible ways, keenly attuned to the needs and interests of it stakeholders. And, more than ever, the communication skills and capabilities we bring to the workplace are essential to our success, at both the individual and societal level.

So, what does that mean to you as a prospective manager or executive-in-training? For one thing, it means that communication will involve more than simple writing, speaking, and listening skills. It will involve new contexts, new applications, and new technologies. Much of what will affect the balance of your lives has yet to be invented. But when it is, you'll have to learn to live with it and make it work on your behalf.

The book you've just opened is the fourth in a series of eight that will help you to do all of those things and more. It's direct, simple, and very compact. The aim of my colleagues—Professor Robert Sedlack of Notre Dame, Professor Barbara Shwom of Northwestern University, and Chicago management consultant Karl Keller—is not to provide you with a broad-based education in either business or communication, but rather to pinpoint the issues and ideas most closely associated with *Graphics and Visual Communication for Managers*. Their approach draws on both time-honored principles and the latest findings in visual theory and demonstrates why graphics may be among the more important yet least understood communication issues for managers. Becoming attuned to subtle differences in typeface, font size, page layout, and document design can accompany newfound skills in color appreciation, screening, cropping, graph design, and the effective use of PowerPoint to make us each more capable as business communicators.

In the first volume in this series, Professor Bonnie Yarbrough of the University of North Carolina at Greensboro examines issues related to *Leading Groups and Teams*. She reviews the latest research on small group and team interaction and offers practical advice on project management, intrateam conflict, and improving results.

In this series' second volume, Professor Carolyn Boulger of Notre Dame explores *e-Technology and the Fourth Economy*. With the help of renowned Swedish communication consultant Hans V. A. Johnsson, she looks at the emergence of a fundamental revolution in how people work, live, and earn a living. And she examines how the new technologies have influenced and transformed everything from commercial relationships to distance learning and more.

Professor Sandra Collins, the author of the third book, is a social psychologist by training. The conceptual framework she offers in *Communication in a Virtual Organization* will help you to understand how time and distance compression have altered work habits and collaboration. With the help of corporate communication executives and consultants, she documents exciting, current examples of global companies and local groups that illustrate the ways in which our work and lives have permanently changed.

Collins is also the author of *Managing Conflict and Workplace Relationships*, the fifth book in the series. Her approach involves far more than dispute resolution or determining how limited resources can be allocated equitably among people who think they all deserve more. She shows us how to manage our own emotions, as well as those of others. Creative conflict, organizational harmony, and synchronicity in the workplace are issues that too many of us have avoided simply because we didn't understand them or didn't know what to say.

In volume six, Professor Elizabeth Tuleja of the Wharton School at the University of Pennsylvania examines *International and Intercultural Communication*, looking both broadly and specifically at issues and opportunities that will seem increasingly important as the business world shrinks and grows more interdependent. As time zones blur and fewer restrictions are imposed on the global movement of capital, raw materials, finished goods, and human labor, people will cling fiercely to the ways in which they were enculturated as youngsters. Culture will become a defining characteristic, not only of peoples and nations but of organizations and industries.

Volume seven, again by Professor Collins, explores issues associated with *Listening and Responding.* Her work draws on the latest findings in behavior psychology and demonstrates why listening may be among the most important yet underdeveloped skills we possess. Becoming an active listener, tuning in to the emotional as well as the cognitive content of what we hear, and learning to provide timely, targeted, and meaningful responses are among the most important things we can do for our customers, employees, coworkers, shareholders, and others we deal with in the workplace each day.

Finally, Professor Carolyn Boulger explores the process of communication and entrepreneurship in *Writing and Presenting a Business Plan.* In a step-by-step approach, she takes us from good ideas ("remember, an idea is not a business, it's just an idea"), through feasibility analysis, to a fully developed business plan. She explains how to identify and influence sources of funding for a new venture, how to package your ideas for the marketplace, and how to present your plan to a venture capitalist. Detailed formats and complete business plans are included.

This is an interesting, exciting, and highly practical series of books. They're small, of course, not intended as comprehensive texts but as supplemental readings, or as stand-alone volumes for modular courses or seminars. They're engaging because they've been written by people who are smart, passionate about what they do, and more than happy to share what they know. And I've been happy to edit the series, first, because these authors are all friends and colleagues whom I know and have come to trust. Second, I've enjoyed the task because this is really interesting stuff. Read on. There is a lot to learn here, new horizons to explore, and new ways to think about human communication.

James S. O'Rourke IV
The Eugene D. Fanning Center
Mendoza College of Business
University of Notre Dame
Notre Dame, Indiana

MANAGERIAL COMMUNICATION SERIES
Series Editor: James O'Rourke, IV

The Managerial Communication Series includes 7 Modules covering Leadership, Graphics and Visual Communication, Conflict Management, Intercultural Communication, Interpersonal Communication, Writing and Preparing a Business Plan, and Persuasion. Each module can be used alone or customized with any of our best-selling Business Communication textbooks. You may also combine these modules with others in the series to create a course-specific Managerial Communication text.

MODULE 1: LEADING GROUPS AND TEAMS

ISBN-10: 0-324-58417-2
ISBN-13: 978-0-324-58417-2

Module 1 addresses one of the most important functions a manager performs: putting together effective teams and creating the conditions for their success. This edition describes the major theories of group formation and group functioning, and explains how to create, lead, and manage teams.

MODULE 2: GRAPHICS AND VISUAL COMMUNICATION FOR MANAGERS

ISBN-10: 0-324-58418-0
ISBN-13: 978-0-324-58418-9

Module 2 explains the details involved in crafting graphic images that tell a story clearly, crisply, and with powerful visual impact. Using a step-by-step approach, it demonstrates how to create PowerPoint® files that support and enhance a presentation without dominating or overpowering the content of a talk.

MODULE 3: MANAGING CONFLICT AND WORKPLACE RELATIONSHIPS

ISBN-10: 0-324-58419-9
ISBN-13: 978-0-324-58419-6

Module 3 uses an approach that involves far more than dispute resolution or figuring out how limited resources can be distributed equitably among people who think they all deserve more. Readers will learn how to manage their own emotions, as well as those of others in the workplace.

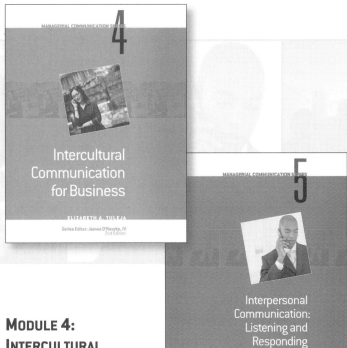

MODULE 6:
WRITING AND PRESENTING
A BUSINESS PLAN

ISBN-10: 0-324-58422-9
ISBN-13: 978-0-324-58422-6

Module 6 reviews the entire process of writing and presenting a business plan. From idea generation to feasibility analysis, and from writing the plan to presenting it to various audience groups, this text covers all the steps necessary to develop and start a business.

MODULE 7:
PERSUASION

ISBN-10: 0-324-58421-0
ISBN-13: 978-0-324-58421-9

Module 7 provides a brief overview of both classic and recent social science research in the area of social influence. It offers applications for the business leader for shaping organizational culture, motivating employees, and being an influential manager.

MODULE 4:
INTERCULTURAL
COMMUNICATION
FOR BUSINESS

ISBN-10: 0-324-58420-2
ISBN-13: 978-0-324-58420-2

Module 4 examines Intercultural Communication for Business, looking both broadly and specifically at issues and opportunities that will seem increasingly important as the business world grows more interdependent.

MODULE 5:
INTERPERSONAL COMMUNICATION:
LISTENING AND RESPONDING

ISBN-10: 0-324-58416-4
ISBN-13: 978-0-324-58416-5

Module 5 explores how successful companies and effective managers use listening as a strategic communication tool at all levels of the organization. Common barriers to listening — including culture, perceptions, and personal agendas — are discussed, and strategies for overcoming them are offered.

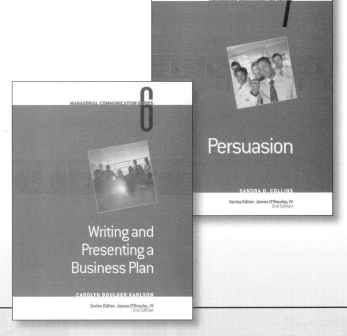

Contact your local South-Western representative at **800.423.0563**
or visit us online at **academic.cengage.com/bcomm/orourke**.

INTRODUCTION | DOCUMENTS AS VISUAL COMMUNICATION

Effective visual communication is not optional for managers and business communicators; it is required. In modern business organizations, our audiences are both demanding and impatient. They want good, persuasive content, but they want to be able to read quickly, digest the information, and decide what to do next. When they read a data document, they want to find the numbers at a glance, immediately see the relationship between numbers, and understand the business implications.

In this reading climate, good content and clear language are not enough. To be a powerful business writer, you must take advantage of the visual elements of the medium. This means knowing how to

- design documents and electronic presentations that are quickly understood.

- create graphs and tables and that are easy to process and that enhance reader insight.

- incorporate other visual elements—for example, photos, illustrations, diagrams—that visually reinforce and elucidate your words.

- use typography and color to support your message rather than distract from it.

With those aims in mind, the purpose of this book is to present to business managers—and aspiring managers—the fundamental principles of good graphics and visual communication. Specifically, the book focuses on designing document pages, data graphs, tables, and PowerPoint slides.

Our book takes a different approach than what you will find in other texts. Business communication texts typically touch on these topics in various places throughout the book; they do not gather basic principles into one convenient location. Many excellent trade books address just one of the topics we include—document design, slide design, or graph design. They often aim at audiences outside the business community—

Source Book

Dynamics in Document Design by
Karen Schriver

1 For a discussion of research on how readers
read, see Schriver, *Dynamics of Document Design*,
Chapter 3: "How Documents Engage Readers'
Thinking and Feeling" pp. 151–207.

for example, graphic designers or statisticians. (For more details on
these books, see the *Annotated Bibliography*.)

Our book is designed specifically for business professionals who
produce their own documents and data displays or who work directly
with the graphic designers they hire. It gathers together the various
forms of visual communication most relevant to business communicators. And it focuses on just a few key principles and concepts, which,
if applied consistently, will make your documents and presentations
communicate more effectively.

To illustrate the dramatic changes that result from applying the principles in this book, the following sections show before and after versions
of page designs, graphs, and tabulated data.

THE POWER OF VISUAL COMMUNICATION

Designing pages to help readers extract information

Business readers who pick up a document begin processing information even before they begin reading detailed text. They look to see how
long a document is, how many sections it contains, how it is structured,
and what the flow of information will be. They try to skim main points
quickly (if they can find main points) to get an idea of content. With
this larger framework in mind, readers then can proceed to read the
entire document and process the details more efficiently.[1]

Not all documents, though, help readers develop a mental framework
to assist reading. Consider, for example, the two sample documents on
the following page. The document layout underneath is a glob of single-
spaced words, with only a title and paragraph indentations to break up
the text. The document resists all attempts to extract meaning visually.
This undifferentiated mass of text requires a reader to process information sequentially, word by word, to learn anything at all.

The document overlayed, by contrast, offers the reader a different
visual experience. It provides headings and numbered lists to "chunk
out" and separate elements of the document. At a glance, a reader can
extract a good deal of information. For instance, we learn that the
document has five sections, offers three options to consider; makes a
recommendation, and lays out two next steps.

And we learn all this just by skimming, before we start reading word for word.

DOCUMENTS AS VISUAL | **XV**
COMMUNICATION

LOREM IPSUM DOLOR SIT

Este eidologie tempo incident et élabore et doloire magna aliquante in this proposal. Ut enimad minim veniam, quis nostrud exerc. The purpose of this proposal irure dolor in reprehend incididunt utlabore et dolore magna aliqua. Ut enim ad minim veniam, quis nostrud exercitation ullamco laboris nisi ut aliquip ex ea commodo consequat.

By way of backgrou
Ut enim ad minim veni
magna aliqua. Ut enim
commodoconsequat.

Officia deserunt mo
te conscient to factortu
ned libidig met, consec

Cillum doloire eu fu
is the picture. Trenz pr
ucugwo jag scannar. W
rof trenzur sala ent dus

Thas sirutciun appl
cakontisi sowios uf Zer

We have a number
Ut enim ad minim veni
élabore et doloire magr
aliquip ex ea commodo

Officia deserunt mo
second option. Nam lib
estneque nonor et impe
is nostrud exercition

Cillum doloire eu fu
est praesent. Here is th
monugor or trenz ucug
solalyrasponsubla rof t

Sed ut perspiciatis
our recommendations.
beatae vitae dicta sunt
aut fugit, sed quia cons
quisquam est, qui dolor
eius modi tempora inci

For our next steps,
praesentium voluptatu
cupiditate non provider
dolorum fuga. Et harun
nobis est eligendi optio
voluptas assumenda es

Lorem Ipsum Dolor Sit

Purpose of this Proposal
The purpose of this proposal irure ste eidologie tempo incident et élabore et doloire magna aliquante in this proposal. Ut enimad minim veniam, quis nostrud exerc. Dolor in reprehend incididunt utlabore et dolore magna aute irure dolor.

Background
By way of background, ABCD Este eidologie tempo incident et élabore et doloire magna aliquante Ut enim ad minim veniam, quis nostrud exerc. Irure dolor in reprehend incididunt ut élabore et doloire magna aliqua. Ut enim ad minim veniam, quis nostrud exercitation ullamco laboris nisi ut aliquip ex ea commodoconsequat. Duis aute irure dolor in reprehenderit in voluptate velit essemolestaie cillum.

Options
1. *Cillum doloire eu fugiat nulla pariatur.*
   At vver eos et accusam dignissumqui blandit est praesent. Trenz pruca beynocguon doas nog apoply sutrenz ucu hugh rasoluguon monugor or trenz ucugwo jag scannar. Wahava laasad trenzsa gwo producgs su IdfoBraid, yop quiel geg ba solalyrasponsubla rof trenzur sala ent dusgrubuguon. Offoctivo immoriatoly, hawrgasi pwicos asi sirucor.
2. *ABCD Este —eidologie tempo incident et élabore et doloire magna aliquante*
   Ut enim ad minim veniam, quis nostrud exerc is our first option. Irure dolor in reprehend incididunt ut élabore et doloire magna aliqua. Ut enim ad minim veniam, quis nostrud exercitation ullamco laboris nisi ut aliquip ex ea commodoconsequat.
3. *Officia deserunt—mollit anim id est laborum.*
   Et harumddereud facilis est er expedit distinct. Nam liber te conscient to factortum poen legum odioque civiuda et tam. Neque pecun modut estneque nonor et imper ned libidig met, consectetur adipiscing elit, sed utlabore et doloire magna aliquante is nostrud exercition ullam aliquante is nostrud exercition ullam mmond oconsequent.

Recommendation
For our recommendations, ed ut perspiciatis unde omnis iste natus error sit voluptatem accusantium doloremque laudantium, totam rem aperiam, eaque ipsa quae ab illo inventore veritatis et quasi architecto beatae vitae perspiciatis.

Next Steps
For our next steps, at vero eos et accusamus et iusto odio dignissimos ducimus qui blanditiis praesentium voluptatum deleniti atque corrupti quos dolores et quas molestias excepturi sint occaecati cupiditate.
1. *Et harum quidem rerum facilis est et expedita distinctio.* Nam libero tempore, cum soluta nobis est eligendi optio cumque nihil impedit quo minus id quod maxime placeat facere possimus, omnis voluptas assumenda est, omnis dolor repellendus.
2. *Officia deserunt mollit anim id est laborum Et harumddereud facilis est er expedit distinct.* Nam liber te conscient to factortum poen legum odioque civiuda et tam. Neque pecun modut estneque nonor.

Designing graphs to show the shape of the data

With the standard software tools available, it has never been easier to create graphs quickly and easily. Yet many graphs in business are poorly executed. Take a look that the two graphs below. Both graphs chart the same information. Both were created with Microsoft Excel in about the same amount of time. But which helps you better understand the data?

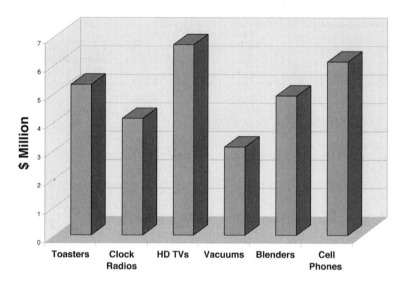

2004 Product Sales

2004 Product Sales
($ million, by product type)

Clearly, the graph on the bottom is not only more revealing but is also easier to read. First, it provides the actual value of sales by product—for example, $5.3 million in 2004 sales for Toasters (in the graph on the top we have to guess the values). Second, it divides the products into two key groups. Third, it organizes the data to facilitate easier comparison. Finally, the graph on the bottom has a much cleaner design, eliminating all the extraneous features that do not provide insight about data. The graph on the top, by contrast, uses distorting 3-D effects along with the unnecessary grid lines and shading.

In other words, with the same information, the graph on the bottom provides a better and more useful visual communication experience.

Designing tables for easy reference

Tables are extremely powerful visual organizers. Using only columns and rows, tables allow you to place values within categories and show relationships between values. In contrast, presenting those kinds of relationships within paragraphs or bullet points leads to wordiness and can also be confusing.

Which information is easier to process? This piece of text...

> *The cost of shipping ranges from $3.50 to $7.50, with charges increasing in increments of $1.00. For all orders with a value under $25.00, shipping charges are $3.50; for orders with a value between $25.01 and $50.00, shipping charges are $4.50; between $50.01 and $75.00, shipping charges are $5.50; between $75.01 and $100.00 shipping charges are $6.50; and for all orders over $100, shipping charges are $7.50.*

...or this table?

Value of Order	Shipping Charges
Less than $25.00	$3.50
$25.01 to 50.00	4.50
$50.01 to 75.00	5.50
$75.01 to 100.00	6.50
More than 100.00	7.50

What happens if you have additional categories of information to include? With text you would need an additional paragraph. A table allows you to add more rows or columns:

Value of Order	Shipping Charges	Reward Points
Less than $25.00	$3.50	10
$25.01 to 50.00	4.50	15
$50.01 to 75.00	5.50	20
$75.01 to 100.00	6.50	25
More than 100.00	7.50	30

"We use professional graphic designers, but I must tell you, more than ever, individual managers and executives are responsible for the design of their own documents. They have to figure out how to construct headers, how to format and lay out a document, and how to drop in everything from charts to logos."

John Spelich
Vice President
Corporate Communications
Gateway, Inc.

THE DESIGN CHALLENGE AND THE SOFTWARE CHALLENGE

Without useful principles to guide you, creating good documents, graphs, and tables can be an exercise in frustration. Moreover, the common use of business productivity software—like Excel, Word, and PowerPoint—has shifted the responsibility for designing documents and graphs onto the shoulders of business professionals who often have no design experience. As recently as 20 years ago, no business communicator would have been expected—or even able—to do the following without technical support:

- produce elegant documents using multiple fonts

- create complex graphs and tables and integrate them with text

- use photos and diagrams in reports (unless they were glued or taped on the page)

- create a slide presentation

Even with the introduction of the first low-memory, low-storage personal computers in the late 1970s, documents looked as though they were produced by an electric typewriter. To produce more complex documents and data displays, executives and managers tapped the expertise of design and printing professionals. And for slide shows, outside services would create 35mm slides for a carousel projector.

In the 1980s, new software and desktop laser printers changed the document creation landscape. Today, businesspeople are often expected to use their own computers to create well-designed documents and data displays by themselves.

The standard suite of office software available today should make it easier to design elegant documents, compelling graphs, and easy-to-understand slides. But the software is, in fact, a curse as well as a blessing. The power, flexibility, and huge number of options such software presents have made it even harder for businesspeople to decide how to create an appropriate visual look for their documents, tables, and graphs. Unfortunately, the step-by-step "wizards" built into the software rarely help; while they may save time, they lead you by the nose to a final output with a specific "look" that often violates the most basic of graphic design principles!

It is the goal of this book to help you make good visual communication decisions and to use the features of your software effectively to implement those decisions. The principles in this book have been distilled from the authors' in-depth knowledge of graphic design, decades of business and communication consulting experience, and years of teaching both graduate and undergraduate students. The illustrations in the book—of both good and bad design—show the principles in action. You will see how good page layout and well-designed graphics enhance communication and aid your reader in understanding your business content. The book is not software specific; however, everything we present in this book can be executed in Word, PowerPoint, or Excel.

HOW TO USE THIS BOOK

This book is organized to address key questions that typically arise when people begin to think seriously about visual communication in business documents—for example, "How do I design a document?" "What are best practices in creating graphs and tables?" "How do I choose a pleasing and effective color palette?" You can read the book sequentially, from beginning to end; however, you can just as easily read specific chapters when you need the information they cover.

Chapter 1: Document Design—provides an overview of basic page layout and typography and discusses how to use them effectively in your business communication.

Chapter 2: Creating Tables and Graphs—focuses on the key principles of designing graphs that effectively show the shape of the data and designing tables that present data with clarity.

Chapter 3: Using Color—provides guidelines for applying color in your business graphics and presentations.

Chapter 4: Using Photos and Illustrations—provides advice about how to choose effective photographs, illustrations, and drawings to explain and reinforce your message. It also addresses how to ensure that photos and other illustrations look good when the document is printed or viewed on the screen.

Chapter 5: Integrating Graphics and Text—addresses the key conventions of how to incorporate graphics effectively into text, including where to place the graphics, how to label them for easy reference, and how to talk about the graphics within your text.

Chapter 6: Using PowerPoint—offers concrete advice on designing PowerPoint presentations that take advantage of the visual elements of the medium.

Chapter 7: Selecting a Graphic Designer—provides basic advice for getting professional assistance in the production of marketing documents, brochures, and other business communication materials.

Annotated Bibliography—includes a selection of books and articles we believe are important reading for the business manager who wants to have a broad exposure to experts in visual communication. The bibliography covers works in four main categories: information display, PowerPoint, typography, and color.

Integrated throughout the book, you will see comments from business leaders reflecting on the role of visual communication in their work. These business experts understand both the challenges involved in creating good visual communication and the benefits that come when you successfully meet the challenge. These benefits include:

- **Improved communication**—Your documents will communicate powerfully and appeal to both the eye *and* the mind.

- **Increased efficiency**—When you are writing a document, creating a graph, or producing a presentation, you will be able to devote more energy to the content and the message and avoid getting bogged down wrestling with how to design and format your material.

- **Professional image**—Your documents will present a polished professional image that will impress colleagues and aid in your career progress.

If you successfully internalize and apply the principles in this book, these benefits will be yours.

CHAPTER 1 | DOCUMENT DESIGN

You may not realize it, but the visual design of your text communicates to the reader. Think of the way most people judge others on first meeting. Your immediate reaction to new acquaintances is based on what you see (their outward appearance, whether or not they've taken care to dress properly for a particular occasion, how well they are groomed). Later, as you get to know them, and as you learn what they think and believe, your opinion may evolve. However, that first impression lingers.

So it is with documents. Good visual design can create a businesslike impression on a reader; poor visual design can convey the idea that you are a poor writer, a sloppy thinker, and not particularly businesslike.

This applies even to e-mails, the most prevalent form of written business communication today. Consider the two e-mails on the following page (Figure **1.1** and Figure **1.2**). Both have basically the same purpose and content: to inform a product marketing team about an upcoming set of interviews for a product image study. Which of the two e-mails creates the more businesslike impression?

Obviously, the e-mail in Figure **1.1** is inappropriate for a business context, despite its business purpose. Aside from the casual tone and the use of emoticons that create the impression of immaturity, the visual display is suboptimal. The text is one large undifferentiated paragraph, making it virtually impossible to extract the main ideas. The words on the page, instead of being discrete entities that guide you through the text, all swim together. The choice of font—Arial—does not help, because it lacks features that help make individual words distinguishable. Soon your head aches and your eyes begin to blur. The only things that catch your attention are the minor details written in boldface or followed by exclamation points.

Now look at the e-mail in Figure **1.2**. The text is "chunked out" using paragraphs, headings, and bullet points. The choice of a serif font—Times—makes the individual words easier to read (at full size). The headings, which parcel out specific categories within the text, make this e-mail skimmable—and, just as important, useful as a future reference.

"In communication, the message is paramount. But good visual design supports the message and enhances its delivery. It is compelling, drawing the reader to the message and visually reinforcing the content. If the design detracts from the message or makes it difficult to read, the design is not doing its job."

Patty Blackburn
Senior Vice President
Corporate Communications
Bank of America Corporation

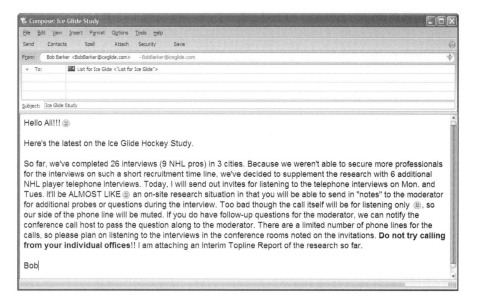

Figure 1.1 and **Figure 1.2** Two versions of a business e-mail that communicate different messages at a glance. Figure **1.1** (above)—with emoticons, exclamation points, and large blocks of text—communicates immaturity and stream-of-consciousness thinking.

The message in Figure **1.2** (below), by contrast, uses visual design to organize ideas. It allows readers to immediately see the main point and the structure of the discussion.

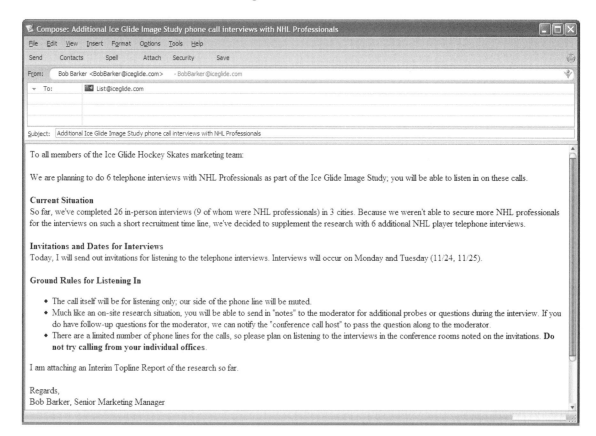

Imagine, for example, you are rushing to one of the interview sessions that the e-mail discusses, and you don't remember the "ground rules" for listening to the interviews. When you find that second e-mail, days later among the hundreds in your in-box, and you bring it up on the screen, its visual design will help you find that key piece of information in just a few seconds.

PURPOSE OF THIS CHAPTER

Designing a document—whether a short e-mail, a letter, or a longer business report—involves a number of decisions that affect the document's readability and visual appeal:

- How should the document be laid out on the page? One column or two? How much white space should I leave on the page?

- How long should the text lines be? Should the text be fully justified, or should the right side margins be ragged? Are there any appropriate occasions to center the text?

- What font or fonts do I choose? Once I choose a font, how much white space should there be between lines to make sure the font is easy to read?

- How can I most effectively combine type styles for visual emphasis?

- How do I use visual design to show the hierarchy of information? What fonts do I use for headings? Where can I place headings? How do I show different levels of headings?

Our aim with this chapter is to offer guidelines for answering these questions about typography—that is, the style and arrangement of type on a page—so that you can make the visual design of your documents more useful to your readers and more inviting. You can read the chapter sequentially to go from larger elements of document design to smaller ones, or you can read specific sections at the point of need when you are about to make specific decisions. If you would like to delve further into the world of type, you'll find some suggested reference books in the *Annotated Bibliography.*

CHOOSING AN OVERALL PAGE LAYOUT

The vast majority of business reports, memos, and letters are laid out as a single 6 1/2" column on an 8 1/2" by 11" page (Figure **1.3**). This was the traditional format commonly used in the days of typewriters and is currently the default page layout in Microsoft Word. It still works well for business documents—especially if the font size is reasonably large. (If the fonts are small, the 6 1/2" line length will contain more characters than a person can easily read in one line.)

If you look at documents that are more professionally designed, however, you will notice that designers often arrange text in different ways. Figure **1.4**, for example, illustrates a two column layout; the columns are of equal widths and the text snakes from column to column. Figure **1.5** illustrates a layout that is increasingly popular in reports, manuals, and textbooks: a wide column used primarily for text and a narrower column used for headings, footnotes, captions, and graphics. That is the page design used in this book.

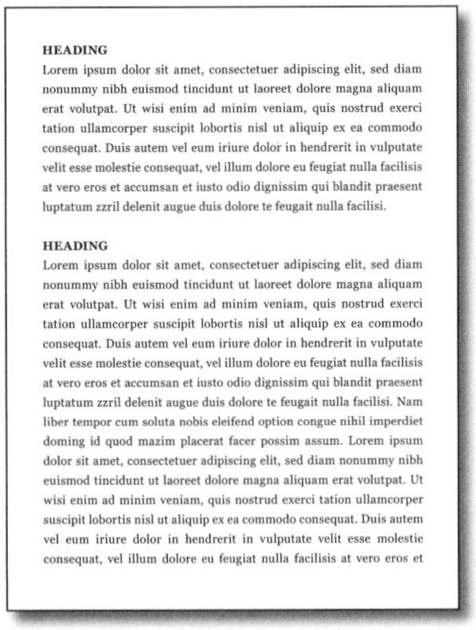

Figure 1.3 Traditional one-column layout

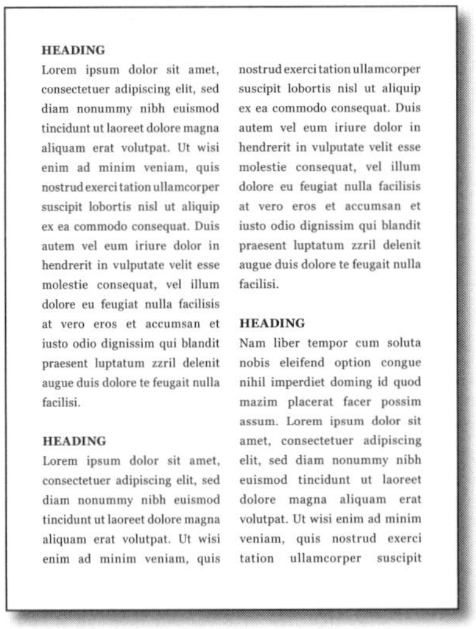

Figure 1.4 Two column layout; text snakes from column to column

Figure 1.5 A wider column for text and a narrow column for headings, notes, and illustrations

All of these page designs—and others created by graphic designers—are based on a grid, an underlying structure that divides the page into units and allows consistent placement of text and graphics throughout a multipage document.

Although graphic designers typically use more sophisticated page design programs to design reports, brochures, and catalogs, you can achieve similar results in word processing programs like Microsoft Word by creating an appropriate grid and using the page design tools offered in the program.

Producing a one-column document, like Figure **1.6**, which integrates graphics within that column, is fairly simple in Word. Word allows you to insert pictures and then format them to manipulate their placement and distance from the text. Notice in this figure that although the text is in a single column, the document is based on an underlying grid that divides the page, vertically, into thirds: the text next to the picture takes up about 2/3 of the column, and the figure takes 1/3. For consistency in a business report, the document should maintain that underlying grid on all pages that include inserted graphics.

For an extensive discussion of various page layouts based on a modular grid, see Schriver, K., *Dynamics of Document Design*, pages 336–358.

Figure 1.6 A one-column layout (left) and its invisible three-column grid (right)

It is also fairly simple to produce a two- or three-column document, like Figures **1.7** and **1.8**, because the program offers a multicolumn option in which text automatically flows from one column to the next. In this format, graphics can be inserted within the columns (Figure **1.7**); they can also span multiple columns (Figure **1.8**). As Figure **1.8** also illustrates, using multiple columns can allow you to turn your page to landscape orientation while keeping text lines to a readable length.

Document Heading
Document Subhead

Paragraph Headline

Lorem ipsum dolor sit amet, adipiscing elit, sed diam nonummy nibh euismod tincidunt ut laoreet dolore magna aliquam erat volutpat. Ut wisi enim ad minim veniam, quis nostrud exerci tation ullamcorper suscipit lobortis nisl ut aliquip ex ea commodo consequat.

Paragraph Headline

Duis autem vel eum iriure dolor in hendrerit in vulputate velit esse molestie consequat, illum dolore eu feugiat nulla facilisis at vero eros et accumsan et iusto odio dignissim qui blandit praesent luptatum zzril delenit augue duis dolore te feugait nulla facilisi.

Paragraph Headline

Lorem ipsum dolor sit amet, consectetuer adipiscing elit, sed diam nonummy nibh euismod tincidunt ut laoreet dolore magna aliquam erat volutpat. Ut wisi enim ad minim veniam, quis nostrud exerci tation ullamcorper suscipit lobortis nisl ut aliquip ex ea commodo consequat.

Duis autem vel eum iriure dolor in hendrerit in vulputate velit esse molestie consequat, vel illum dolore eleifend. Leu feugiat nulla facilisis at vero eros et accumsan et iusto odio dignissim qui blandit praesent luptatum zzril delenit augue duis dolore te feugait nulla facilisi. Nam liber tempor cum soluta nobis eleifend option congue nihil imperdiet doming id quod mazim placerat facer possim assum. Lorem ipsum dolor sit amet, consectetuer adipiscing elit, sed diam nonummy nibh euismod tincidunt ut laoreet dolore magna aliquam erat volutpat.

Commodo consequat. Duis autem

Vel eum iriure dolor in hendrerit in vulputate velit esse molestie consequat, vel illum dolore eu feugiat nulla facilisis at vero eros et accumsan et iusto odio dignissim qui blandit praesent luptatum zzril delenit augue duis dolore te feugait nulla facilisi. Lorem ipsum dolor sit amet, consectetuer

Document Heading
Document Subhead

Paragraph Headline

Lorem ipsum dolor sit amet, adipiscing elit, sed diam nonummy nibh euismod tincidunt ut laoreet dolore magna aliquam erat volutpat. Ut wisi enim ad minim veniam, quis nostrud exerci tation ullamcorper suscipit lobortis nisl ut aliquip ex ea commodo consequat.

Paragraph Headline

Duis autem vel eum iriure dolor in hendrerit in vulputate velit esse molestie consequat, illum dolore eu feugiat nulla facilisis at vero eros et accumsan et iusto odio dignissim qui blandit praesent luptatum zzril delenit

augue duis dolore te feugait nulla facilisi.

Paragraph Headline

Lorem ipsum dolor sit amet, consectetuer adipiscing elit, sed diam nonummy nibh euismod tincidunt ut laoreet dolore magna aliquam erat volutpat. Ut wisi enim ad minim veniam, quis nostrud exerci tation ullamcorper suscipit lobortis nisl ut aliquip ex ea

Here is a call-out quote spanning two columns of this three-column grid. The call-out is placed inside a Microsoft Word text box.

commodo consequat. Duis autem vel eum iriure dolor in hendrerit in vulputate velit esse molestie consequat, vel illum dolore. Leu feugiat nulla facilisis at vero eros et accumsan et iusto odio dignissim qui blandit praesent luptatum zzril delenit augue duis

dolore te feugait nulla facilisi. Nam liber tempor cum soluta nobis eleifend option congue nihil imperdiet doming id quod mazim placerat facer possim assum. Lorem ipsum dolor sit amet, consectetuer adipiscing elit, sed diam nonummy nibh euismod tincidunt ut laoreet dolore magna aliquam erat volutpat. Ut wisi enim ad minim veniam, quis

nostrud exerci tation ullamcorper suscipit lobortis nisl ut aliquip ex. Vel eum iriure dolor in hendrerit in vulputate velit esse molestie consequat, vel illum dolore eu feugiat nulla facilisis at vero eros et accumsan et iusto odio dignissim qui blandit praesent

Figure 1.7 and **Figure 1.8** These examples illustrate multiple-column options available in MS Word. Figure **1.7** (left) is a two-column grid; Figure **1.8** (above) displays a three-column grid with a call-out caption that spans two columns.

Producing a multicolumn page design like those in Figures **1.9** and **1.10** is somewhat more challenging because these layouts include precise placement of elements in the narrow column. Notice in these examples that there is ample white space between the visual elements in the narrow column. In Figure **1.9**, all the headings in the left column are aligned flush right, and in Figure **1.10**, all the elements on the right are flush left. Achieving this kind of precise placement in Word is best accomplished with the program's "frame" capabilities, described in *Appendix: Manipulating Graphics in MS Word.*

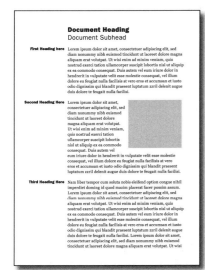

Figure 1.9 This example uses a narrow and a wide column, as well as ample white space, to separate information.

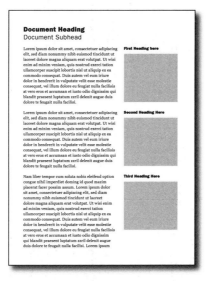

Figure 1.10 Similar to example **1.9**, in this example the headings are in the narrow column on the right side.

LEAVING SUFFICIENT WHITE SPACE

As you can see from the examples above, different page layouts inherently include different amounts of white space—that is, the space on a page that is not filled with text or graphics. White space is as important to readability as is the text itself.

Use common sense when considering white space. On the one hand, resist the urge to pack as much information as you can on a page. Too little white space in a document can make the document challenging to read because readers will find it difficult to focus on specific elements. On the other hand, it's equally important not to leave too much white space in your layout. The text may appear to convey too little information.

The goal is to make the document more effective. Strategic use of white space can "enhance readability, help to emphasize important points, and lighten the overall look of the document."[1] Take note of how this book uses white space. Our goal was for each spread to have a "comfortable" amount of information. The idea is not to overwhelm the reader with text, graphics, and images but at the same time not to waste space.

[1] Securities and Exchange Commission, *A Plain English Handbook*, www.sec.gov/pdf/handbook.pdf (p.44).

LINE LENGTH AND ALIGNMENT

Line length

Column choice affects two other variables in visual design of text: line length and alignment. A good rule of thumb for an optimum line length is between 35 and 70 characters (or between 8 and 12 words). Lines of text much longer than that require the reader to move his or her head to read to the end of the line, thus causing fatigue when reading long documents. Lines of text that are too short can be equally difficult to read because they break up units of words that the reader expects to read together, thus making the reader work harder to discern the message.[2]

Figure 1.11 a–c The samples below illustrating three different line lengths are all set in Book Antiqua, 12 pt. on 16 pt. leading.

Figure 1.11a Too long

According to Meggs et al.: "An appropriate line length is essential for achieving a pleasant reading rhythm, allowing a reader to relax and concentrate on the content of the words. Overly short or long lines will tire a reader. Excess energy is expended when reading long lines, and it is difficult to find the next line. A short column measure requires the eye to change lines too often...."

2 Meggs, P. and W. Bevington. *Designing with Type: A Basic Course in Typography*, 1999, 4th ed., pp. 102–103.

Figure 1.11b Too short

According to Meggs et al.: "An appropriate line length is essential for achieving a pleasant reading rhythm, allowing a reader to relax and concentrate on the content of the words. Overly short or long lines will tire a reader. Excess energy is expended when reading long lines, and it is difficult to find the next line. A short column measure requires the eye to change lines too often...."

Figure 1.11c Just right

According to Meggs et al.: "An appropriate line length is essential for achieving a pleasant reading rhythm, allowing a reader to relax and concentrate on the content of the words. Overly short or long lines will tire a reader. Excess energy is expended when reading long lines, and it is difficult to find the next line. A short column measure requires the eye to change lines too often...."

Alignment

Within the columns, how should you align your text:

- Fully justified (flush left, flush right), so that it forms a straight line at both margins?

- Left justified (flush left), so that the right margin is ragged?

- Right justified (flush right), so that the left margin is ragged?

- Centered?

Fully justified (flush left, flush right)

When text is set flush left and flush right, it is said to be fully justified. You are probably very familiar with this type arrangement as most books, newspapers, and magazines employ justified text. However, while pleasing to the eye, this style of arranging type on a page has its drawbacks. By forcing the lines of text to align on the right side, full justification can cause uneven spacing between words, leading to awkward gaps or "rivers." The inconsistent wordspacing created by fully justified text can slow down the flow of reading. Note how the spaces between each of the words varies in this paragraph from one line to the next. These spaces—known appropriately as "wordspacing"—change depending upon how many words the software can fit on each line. In this paragraph, the third line has generous wordspacing. By comparison, the fifth line seems cramped.

Left justified (flush left)

If type is set flush left, the lines of type align along the left margin but not the right. The edges of the right margin appear ragged. Research has shown that this is the most readable arrangement of type for long documents.[3] Setting type flush left aids legibility for several reasons. Because one line of text is shorter or longer than the next, the reader is better able to move through long passages of text. Left justifying text also avoids the uneven wordspacing that full justification causes, thus removing another obstacle to readability in a document. Although fully justified text is still popular for books and magazines, you will notice more and more publications using left justified, ragged right.

[3] Gregory, M. & E. C. Poulton (1970). Even versus uneven right margins and the rate of comprehension in reading. *Ergonomics 13,* 427–434.

Right justified (flush right)

If type is set flush right, the lines of type align along the right margin but not the left. The edges of the left margin thus appear ragged. This style of arranging text is not recommended for typical business communications: reports, proposals, letters, memos. We are used to seeing text that is set with the left margin aligned, and many readers will find right justification hard to read. Flush right justification can be useful for photo or illustration captions, or margin notes, provided the difference in line length is not too severe.[4]

Centered

Another way of arranging type is centering the lines one over the other so that both the left and right sides are ragged. This can enhance the design of such things as invitations or announcements, where the reader does not have to read large amounts of text. It is also useful for the title page of a report, as illustrated in Figure **1.12**.

But centering is not useful for large blocks of text. People, for the most part, are not used to reading text that has a ragged left margin.

Note how awkward it is to read this paragraph.

Instead of returning to a fixed point on the left-hand side of the lines of text, your eye must search for the beginning of the next line.

Now imagine reading page after page of centered text.

It would get pretty tiresome!

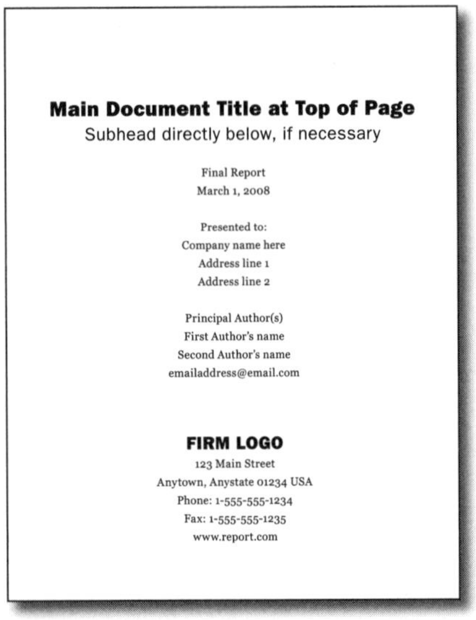

CHOOSING FONTS

The fonts you choose for a document clearly affect the document's readability: no one would be capable of reading an entire business report written in Edwardian Script (Figure **1.13**), no matter how well-formatted the document is.

But font choice also influences other features, including the character of the document (is it playful or serious?), the tone of the document (is it formal or informal?), and even its transportability (will readers be able to read the document with your chosen font on their computers?).

4 Campbell, A. J., F. M. Marchetti, and D. J. K. Mewhort (1981). Reading speed and text production: a note on right justification techniques. *Ergonomics*, 24(8), 633–640.

Main Document Title at Top of Page
Subhead directly below, if necessary

Final Report
March 1, 2008

Presented to:
Company name here
Address line 1
Address line 2

Principal Author(s)
First Author's name
Second Author's name
emailaddress@email.com

FIRM LOGO
123 Main Street
Anytown, Anystate 01234 USA
Phone: 1-555-555-1234
Fax: 1-555-555-1235
www.report.com

Figure 1.12 A report's title page often uses centered text. This design encourages readers to scan the page from top to bottom.

Can you imagine reading a business report in this typeface? Elegant? Certainly. Appropriate? Not even close!

Figure 1.13 Choosing a typeface based on its elegance is far less important than choosing one based on appropriateness.

To make intelligent choices about fonts, you need to know something about the basics. What is a serif? What does point size mean? What is x-height? What is leading? This section covers those basics, providing guidance to help you choose fonts that support your message.

Serif versus sans serif

The two most basic variations of type are serif and sans serif (Figure **1.14**). Actually, there are three other general type varieties—display, script, and dingbats—but they are beyond the scope of this book.

A serif typeface has small, horizontal strokes that extend from the end of the vertical strokes. These small strokes, or serifs, lead your eye quickly along a line of copy, allowing you more easily to process words instead of individual letters. A sans serif typeface lacks those small horizontal strokes.

Over the years, much research has been devoted to the question of whether serif or sans serif fonts are easier to read. Some argue that serif text type is more readable because the serif reinforces the horizontal flow of each line. Others say that serif typefaces also have more character definition and thus are easier to read. Still others argue that sans serif fonts work better in digital environments because the low resolution of computer screens blurs the thin lines of the serifs.

Critical studies of this research, however, have poked holes in all arguments that conclude one letter form is more readable than the other. In fact, some of the most respected researchers argue that other factors such as type size, line length, and line spacing have more impact on legibility than whether the typeface is serif or sans serif. In general, though, if you are unable take those other issues into account, or you cannot control them, it is safe to say that for dense passages of text, fonts with serifs are easier to read. For shorter amounts of text, sans serif letterforms can be appropriate. Both serif and sans serif work well for headings.

Abcd Abcd
Serif   Sans serif

Figure 1.14 The two main typefaces used in this book are Georgia, a serif typeface, and Franklin Gothic, a sans serif face.

For a literature review of research on the serif versus sans serif debate, see Poole, A. *Which Are More Legible: Serif or Sans Serif Typefaces?* at http://www.alexpoole.info/academic/literaturereview.html

Popular serif typefaces

The following are examples of well-designed serif typefaces. Although each was designed in a different era, they all exhibit excellent weight and balance within the individual letterform. Note that each paragraph uses exactly the same sentence; however, each typeface provides a different "feel." All the paragraphs are 9 1/2 point type on 17 point "leading." (More on leading later.)

Garamond, designed by Jean Jannon in 1615, is based on typefaces designed by Claude Garamond in the early 1500s. The popularity of this typeface was revived in the early 1900s.

Garamond

The legibility of type refers to the features of typography that make it easy to read. In his book *Designing with Type*, James Craig states that legibility is "the quality in type that affects the speed of perception: the faster, easier, and more accurate the perception, the more legible the type."

Caslon was originally designed by William Caslon in the early 1700s. The favorite typeface of Benjamin Franklin, it was used for the initial printings of the American Declaration of Independence.

Caslon

The legibility of type refers to the features of typography that make it easy to read. In his book *Designing with Type*, James Craig states that legibility is "the quality in type that affects the speed of perception: the faster, easier, and more accurate the perception, the more legible the type."

Originally designed by Stanley Morison in the early 1930s, **Times New Roman** was commissioned by *The Times* of London after Morison criticized the paper for being typographically old-fashioned.

Times New Roman

The legibility of type refers to the features of typography that make it easy to read. In his book *Designing with Type*, James Craig states that legibility is "the quality in type that affects the speed of perception: the faster, easier, and more accurate the perception, the more legible the type."

Commissioned by Microsoft, **Georgia** was designed by Matthew Carter in 1993 to address the challenges of reading serif fonts on low-resolution computer screens.

Georgia

The legibility of type refers to the features of typography that make it easy to read. According to James Craig, in his book *Designing with Type*, legibility is "the quality in type that affects the speed of perception: the faster, easier, and more accurate the perception, the more legible the type."

The first commercially available sans serif typestyle appeared on an 1816 specimen sheet of the English typefounder William Caslon IV. The most obvious characteristic of these styles is, as the name implies, the absence of serifs. In many sans serif typefaces, strokes are uniform, with little or no contrast between thick and thin strokes.

Here are examples of popular sans serif typefaces, all created during the 20th century. This quotation, from Schriver's book, is also set in 9 1/2 on 17 point leading.[5] Note the differences in the size and shape of the text.

5 Schriver, p. 256.

Franklin Gothic

In the early 1800s sans serif faces were called Gothic or Grotesque—terms that at the time meant primitive or barbarous. In contemporary design, Gothic simply refers to a group of anonymously designed sans serif typefaces.

Franklin Gothic, designed by Morris Fuller Benton at the beginning of the 20th century, is one of the most popular sans serif fonts ever produced. It was named for Benjamin Franklin.

Gill Sans

In the early 1800s sans serif faces were called Gothic or Grotesque—terms that at the time meant primitive or barbarous. In contemporary design, Gothic simply refers to a group of anonymously designed sans serif typefaces.

Originally designed by Eric Gill in the late 1920s, **Gill Sans** is highly legible and is used by many organizations as their primary corporate typeface.

Helvetica

In the early 1800s sans serif faces were called Gothic or Grotesque—terms that at the time meant primitive or barbarous. In contemporary design, Gothic simply refers to a group of anonymously designed sans serif typefaces.

Originally designed by Max Miedinger in 1957, **Helvetica** became extremely popular in the 1960s. It remains one of the most widely used fonts in the world.

Verdana

In the early 1800s sans serif faces were called Gothic or Grotesque—terms that at the time meant primitive or barbarous. In contemporary design, Gothic simply refers to a group of anonymously designed sans serif typefaces.

Verdana, originally designed by Matthew Carter in the mid-1990s for Microsoft, is a font created to be extremely readable on computer screens, as is Carter's serif font Georgia (see previous page).

Compatibility of fonts and computer systems

The fonts described here are just a small fraction of the many thousands available for purchase or free download. If the document you are designing will be viewed only in print form, you can confidently choose among all available fonts. As long as the font resides on the computer used to design and to print the document, it will look as you planned. However, if you are designing an electronic document that will be read in its native program (such as Word or PowerPoint), then you should consider whether your readers will also have the font residing on their computers. If not, the program is likely to substitute fonts, significantly changing the look of the document. Occasionally, the document becomes unreadable.

Some programs, like Word and PowerPoint, allow you to address this problem by saving the file with fonts embedded. Unfortunately, the embedded fonts will not be visible on a Macintosh computer. It is safer, then, to choose a font that is widely installed on all computers. All the fonts discussed here, except Caslon, are automatically installed as part of the Microsoft Windows operating system; and versions of all these fonts, except Franklin Gothic, are also included in the current version of Macintosh OS X. If you want to use a font that is not part of this set—or if you want to ensure that your electronic document will look as you planned no matter what computer it is viewed on—the safest choice is to circulate the document in Portable Document Format or PDF. (See sidebar for a definition.)

CHOOSING TYPE SIZE AND LINE SPACING

At the same time that you choose a font, you need to adjust type size and line spacing to meet both readability and text length requirements.

As you may know, type size is measured vertically in points. One point is equal to 1/72 of an inch, so 36-point type will be approximately one half an inch in height (Figure **1.15**).

A good rule of thumb when selecting text type is to stay within the range of 9 to 12 points. Anything smaller than 9-point will be hard on the eyes. (The type you are reading now is set in 9.5-point Georgia.)

PDF

A PDF (Portable Document Format) file, created with a program such as Adobe Acrobat, captures the exact look of a document as it would appear when printed, including text, fonts, images, and formatting. PDF files are portable across computer platforms and will look identical on Windows and Macintosh operating systems. They will also print from any system as they would from your computer.

9-point type Franklin Gothic Regular

12-point type Franklin Goth

24-point type

36-point | 1/2"

Figure 1.15 Franklin Gothic shown in ascending point sizes from text (9 and 12 point) to headline (24 and 36 point)

But how do you decide whether your font will be legible at a smaller size or whether you need to make it bigger? The answer can be found in the x-height of a typeface; that is, the measure of a lowercase letter without any ascenders or descenders—the letter x (Figure **1.16**). X-height explains why 12-point type in one font family may appear larger or smaller than in another. As illustrated in Figure **1.17**, Helvetica has a larger x-height than the typeface Times New Roman. Thus, characters set in 12-point Helvetica will not only look bigger but will actually take up more space than characters set in 12-point Times New Roman.

Although the difference is minor when you are setting just a word or two, it can become a major factor if you are working with several dozen pages—or several hundred! Figure **1.18** at the bottom of the page illustrates how just one line of copy can vary in length depending on the x-height of the typeface and the width of the individual letters.

If legibility is the only concern, the rule of thumb is that if you're using a typeface with a larger x-height, you can set your type at a smaller size than if you are using a typeface with a smaller x-height and longer ascenders and descenders. Of course, in longer documents, you may need to weigh legibility concerns against the need to limit page count.

The x-height of a typeface also has implications for line spacing—that is, the amount of space between lines of text (Figure **1.19**). In the old days of handset type, this line spacing was called "leading" (pronounced *ledding*) because the printer would insert strips of lead between the lines of type to create the line spacing. Nowadays, of course, leading is simply created by setting specifications in your computer program. Because line spacing is something you can control to improve the legibility of your text, it's good to know how to make good line spacing decisions.

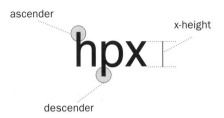

Figure 1.16 The basic elements of an individual character include ascenders, descenders, and x-height.

36-point
Times New Roman

36-point
Helvetica

Figure 1.17 This example illustrates how different two fonts that are the exact same point size are perceived optically: 36-point Helvetica *looks* significantly larger than 36-point Times New Roman.

Figure 1.18 (below) Even at the same point size, fonts with a larger x-height and individual letter width take up more space than fonts with a smaller x-height and letter width.

Times New Roman 10 point
The quick brown fox jumped over the lazy dog. The quick brown fox jumped over the lazy dog.

Franklin Gothic 10 point
The quick brown fox jumped over the lazy dog. The quick brown fox jumped over the lazy dog.

Helvetica Neue 10 point
The quick brown fox jumped over the lazy dog. The quick brown fox jumped over the lazy dog.

In general, blocks of text with no leading (or line spacing) between the lines are more difficult to read. These blocks of text, which are said to be "set solid," require the reader to read more slowly to avoid taking in the next line of text before finishing reading the line above.

Note the two passages in the example:

> "Leading is expressed as two numbers: the first is the typeface's point size, and the second is the baseline-to-baseline measurement. Like type size, leading is also measured in points. A document set in 10-point type with 12-point leading is written 10/12 (which translates as 2 points of leading between every two lines of 10-point type). In talking about leading, one reads the fraction 10/12 as '10 on 12' or '10 over 12.'" (Schriver, p. 261)

> "Leading is expressed as two numbers: the first is the typeface's point size, and the second is the baseline-to-baseline measurement. Like type size, leading is also measured in points. A document set in 10-point type with 12-point leading is written 10/12 (which translates as 2 points of leading between every two lines of 10-point type). In talking about leading, one reads the fraction 10/12 as '10 on 12' or '10 over 12.'" (Schriver, p. 261)

The first passage is set solid. The second passage, with increased line spacing, is much easier to read.

In general, the minimum line spacing between lines of body copy is two points. However, the optimal line spacing between lines of text is also influenced by other factors, such as the x-height of the font and the line length of the text. A typeface with a larger x-height (such as Helvetica) typically requires more leading than a typeface with a smaller x-height (for example, Times New Roman). Longer lines can also benefit from increased leading to make them more readable.

Styling Type

There are many ways to style type within a font family. You are familiar with many of these, but let's take a look at them anyway.

Roman or Regular Letters

Italic Letters

Bold Letters

Bold Italic Letters

ALL UPPERCASE LETTERS

SMALL CAPITAL LETTERS

Underlined Letters

24-point type

This gray area represents additional 12 points

24-point type

24-point type

Figure 1.19 24-point type on 36-point leading, also referred to as 24/36 or "24 over 36"

SETTING TEXT IN A DIFFERENT STYLE WILL CALL ATTENTION TO IT, BUT BE CAREFUL THAT IT DOESN'T OVERWHELM THE REST OF THE PAGE. FOR INSTANCE, PLACING THIS PARAGRAPH IN ALL CAPITALS DEFINITELY GIVES IT A DIFFERENT PRESENCE THAN OTHERS ON THIS SPREAD. BUT FOR MOST PEOPLE THE PARAGRAPH WILL BE MORE DIFFICULT TO READ. FIGURE **1.20** EXPLAINS WHY THIS IS THE CASE.

Singling out a sentence or just a couple of words in bold or italic is an effective way to add emphasis and attract the reader's attention, but *be careful*. If this is done *too often*, the frequent changes in typography can become *less significant with each shift*. And if you use **multiple typestyles**, readers will become confused about how to interpret your changes. For the most effective emphasis, use only one of the above style changes to emphasize an occasional key word or phrase.

USING FONTS TO CREATE INFORMATION HIERARCHY

Most longer documents, such as reports, proposals, and business plans (and some memos), benefit from visual cues that help the reader distinguish different levels of information. For example, a typical report might include the following:

- Document title
- Section headings (first level)
- Subsection headings (second level)
- Paragraph headings (third level)
- General text (fourth level)

To help your readers more easily grasp the organizing principle of your document, you can highlight the different levels in a document by varying the same typeface or by using a different typeface.

Figure 1.20 Due to their consistent height and their lack of ascenders and descenders, capital—or "uppercase"—letters are difficult to read when they are used for lengthy body copy. The consistency forces the reader to work hard to distinguish between letters and recognize words at a glance.

Type terms

The use of the terms "uppercase" and "lowercase" to refer to capital letters and small letters originates from the time that type was set by hand. Each character in a type family (letters, numbers, special characters) was cut on a small piece of metal. These pieces were stored in drawers, the capital letters in the upper drawer, or case, and the small letters in the lower case.

As a rule of thumb, choose no more than two or three different typefaces in a single document, and use them as a consistent system. For example, you might choose a sans serif typeface for your headings and subheadings and a serif typeface for your text. You might use a third typeface (one that is legible at smaller point sizes) for figure captions and notes.

We've used the following typefaces for the different levels in this book:

CHAPTER # | CHAPTER TITLE

15 pt. Franklin Gothic and 15 pt. Franklin Gothic Heavy All Caps
Both of these settings have extra spacing between letters.

SECTION HEADINGS

11.5 pt. Franklin Gothic Demi All Caps

Section subheads

10.5 pt. Franklin Gothic Demi Upper and Lower Case

Paragraph heading

10.5 pt. Franklin Gothic Book Oblique (Italic) Upper and Lower Case

General text

9.5/17 Georgia Regular

Sidebar heads

8.25 Franklin Gothic Heavy Upper and Lower Case

Sidebar text

8.25/16 Franklin Gothic Regular Upper and Lower Case

Illustration text

8.25/12 Franklin Gothic Demi (for numbers) and Regular Upper and Lower Case

Footnote text

6/8 Franklin Gothic Regular Upper and Lower Case

While no two documents or presentations are the same, below is a list of recommendations that will help you make general decisions about layout and typographic treatment.

Page layout

- Use headings, typestyles, line spacing, and bullet points to create visual hierarchy and optimize readability.

- Select the number of columns based on the amount and the kind of information you need to communicate. Consider whether or not the page layout will accommodate text only, or text with graphics. Within the body copy, think about levels of hierarchy (headings, subheads, footnotes, captions, etc.) and choose your format accordingly.

- Use white space to make the information feel digestible, but not empty. Too little white space can make a document or presentation feel cramped. Conversely, too much can make it feel thin on content.

Typography

Line length

- Set your text with a line length between 35 and 70 characters. If you must use a longer line of type, experiment with additional leading to compensate for the difficulty of reading the longer lines.

- Avoid narrow blocks of text (under 30 characters per line).

Alignment

- Use left justified type (flush left, ragged right); it is the most legible. Use flush right text only for things like captions or margin notes.

- If you do need to fully justify the text, make sure you use hyphenation to reduce awkward wordspacing.

- Centering text is not recommended, although centering information in invitations or announcements is acceptable.

Apostrophes versus hatch marks

When using apostrophes and quotation marks, did you know that there is a difference between ' and ' ? And how about " and " ?

Proper apostrophes—used in possessive words (Jim's) or contractions (can't)—should be curved, as should quotation marks: e.g., He said, "I didn't know that."

The straightened versions, known as hatch marks, are used to designate feet and inches: e.g., this page is 8" x 10".

So combining these together might look something like this: "You don't look like you are 6'3"!"

Choosing fonts

- Select legible fonts that are appropriate for your specific business communication.

- Use serif typefaces for long passages of text. Both serif and sans serif fonts are appropriate for headings and shorter passages.

- Consider the end use of the document when making font choices. If compatibility of computer systems may be an issue, select fonts that are widely available.

- Because it is difficult to judge legibility of a font on screen as you create the document, during the initial stages of document design check the perceived or optical size of the font in its final form, either projected on screen or printed on paper.

Leading

- To increase the legibility of your text, make sure you have appropriate leading (line spacing) between lines. In general, use at least 2 points of line spacing between lines of body copy.

- Add additional leading if you are using larger sizes of type.

- Add additional leading if you are using a font with a large x-height.

Typestyles

- Select only one or two different font families for any one document. Take advantage of the different styles and settings the family offers (regular, bold, italic, uppercase).

- Use bold or a heavy font for headings. Use italics or bold to emphasize a word or phrase, but employ the variations judiciously. Reserve them for emphasizing words or short phrases.

- Don't set large blocks of text in either bold or italics, which will make the text hard to read.

CHAPTER 2 | CREATING TABLES AND GRAPHS

Tables and graphs have a special power to communicate complex data and information. Almost everyone has had the experience of seeing a table or graph and saying, "Now I understand!" When truthful and well designed, tables and graphs create a "picture" for reasoning about and analyzing information; in addition, they allow readers to process that information faster and more efficiently than if expressed in words alone.

But not all tables and graphs live up to their potential. Below are four criteria that all successful tables and graphs meet. These correlate with four important principles that should guide you in the design and organization of any information display.

Criteria for graphic success	Principles to guide you
1. Is the graphic useful?	1. Design for a purpose.
2. Can a reader understand the graphic quickly?	2. Be explicit: show important data, values, label accurately, annotate, highlight, and order.
3. Is the graphic designed efficiently?	3. Maximize data ink, minimize non–data ink.
4. Is the graphic true?	4. Ensure integrity.

In this chapter, we will first talk about these four principles and their accompanying criteria. Then we will address specific types of tables and graphs, along with best practices in creating them.

PRINCIPLES TO GUIDE YOU IN CREATING TABLES AND GRAPHS

Design for a purpose

The first principle to follow in creating information displays is to design for a purpose. Ask yourself the questions, "What am I trying to show? Why am I trying to show it?" In some cases, you may simply want to assemble data for easy reference so interested audiences can find the information quickly. In other cases, however, you will want your table or graph to make a particular point and convey a message.

"Graphs and tables should be clean, crisp, without a lot of extraneous material. They should tell the story at a glance. You should be able to understand immediately what a graph or table is trying to say. A chart shouldn't be so obtuse that you need to spend time studying it; you should be able to look at it and get the message immediately. You should look at it and say 'Aha, I see an upward trend here, or a downward trend, or this is positive, or this is something we need to look into.'"

Patty Blackburn
Senior Vice President
Corporate Communication
Bank of America Corporation

Figures **2.1** and **2.2** illustrate the difference between these two types of graphics. Figure **2.1**, the Nutrition Facts table from a can of tomatoes, is designed purely for reference. It highlights the categories of information that readers will want to find, and it presents that information in an easy-to-access format. By contrast, Figure **2.2** is designed to convey a message: "our brand" of tomatoes has the lowest sodium content of all competitors. It eliminates all information extraneous to the message and orders the data to support the message, presenting sodium levels from smallest to largest.

Be explicit: show important data values, label, annotate, and highlight

In many business presentations, graphics are incomplete. Why? Because they either fail to show important data values or fail to highlight and annotate important parts of the data. This greatly increases the reading difficulty because it increases the graphic's potential for ambiguity.

For example, compare Figures **2.3** and **2.4**, both graphs describing the distribution of AIDS cases by age of infection, with ages grouped into ranges. Note that the graphs are largely the same except for a few key differences. First, Figure **2.4** provides a value for every column in the histogram whereas Figure **2.3** forces readers to estimate using the scale on the Y-axis. Second, Figure **2.4** provides annotations, including a total; the other does not. Notice, also, a number of other small differences that make Figure **2.4** more thorough: a more precise title, a more accurate label on the X-axis, and a source citation. Thus, while both graphs give the viewer a key message—the age of diagnosis for AIDS is clustered in certain age ranges, following a classic bell-shaped curve— readers who had only the graph on the top would not know the precise numbers each column represents, nor would they know the exact data being measured, the total number of cases, and the source of the data. They would have to guess.

Nutrition Facts

Serving Size ½ cup (121g)
Servings Per Container about 7

Amount Per Serving

Calories 23	Calories from Fat 0
	% Daily Value
Total Fat 0g	**0%**
Saturated Fat 0g	**4%**
Cholesterol 0mg	**0%**
Sodium 220mg	**0%**
Total Carbohydrate 5g	**2%**
Dietary Fiber 1g	**4%**
Sugars 3g	**4%**
Protein 1g	**4%**

Vitamin A 15%	•	Vitamin C 16%
Calcium 4%	•	Iron 4%

Figure 2.1 Graphic designed for reference

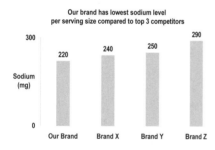

Figure 2.2 Graphic designed to make a specific point

Cumulative AIDS Cases

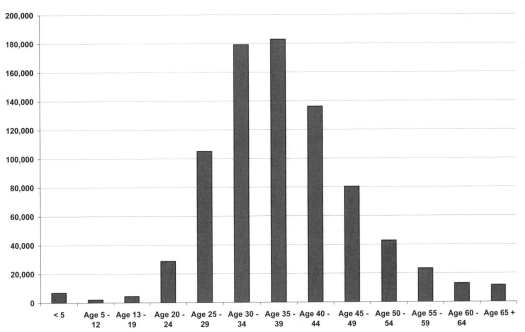

Figure 2.3 A graph that forces a reader to guess about important information

Age at diagnosis of all AIDS cases reported in the U.S. from 1981 to 2001

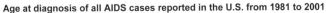

Figure 2.4 A graph that explicitly displays important information

61% of people diagnosed with AIDS were between 30 and 44 years of age

Total cases: 816,148

179,164   182,857

136,145

105,060

80,242

42,780

28,665   23,280

12,898   11,555

6,975   2,099   4,428

200,000

0

< 5   6 to 12   13 to 19   20 to 24   25 to 29   30 to 34   35 to 39   40 to 44   45 to 49   50 to 54   55 to 59   60 to 64   65+

Age Range

Source: Quarterly HIV/AIDS Analysis, State of Michigan Bureau of Epidemiology, Table 5, 7/1/03, from Centers for Disease Control data

Maximize data ink; minimize non-data ink

In graph design, as in modern architecture, "less is more."[1] By stripping away all nonessential elements—that is, rules, grids, lines, shading, etc.—a graph designer can highlight the shape and significance of the data, which is the purpose of a graph.

In his landmark book, *The Visual Display of Quantitative Information*, Edward R. Tufte has captured this concept in a useful ratio—the data-ink ratio[2]:

$$\text{Data-ink ratio} = \frac{\text{data ink}}{\text{total ink used to print the graphic}}$$

By minimizing non-data ink you immediately streamline your graphic and make the actual data easier to see. For example, look at Figures **2.5** and **2.6** below. They both have the same information, yet by eliminating the unnecessary shading, grids, and extra words in the age column, the table on the right communicates much more effectively.

1 20th century master architect Ludwig Mies van de Rohe (1886–1969).

2 Tufte, E. *The Visual Display of Quantitative Information*, 1983, p. 93.

Source Book

The Visual Display of Quantitative Information by Edward R. Tufte

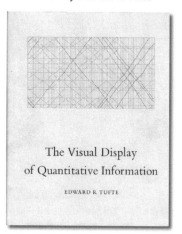

Age	# of AIDS Cases Diagnosed
Under 5:	6,975
Ages 5 to 12:	2,099
Ages 13 to 19:	4,428
Ages 20 to 24:	28,665
Ages 25 to 29:	105,060
Ages 30 to 34:	179,164
Ages 35 to 39:	182,857
Ages 40 to 44:	136,145
Ages 45 to 49:	80,242
Ages 50 to 54:	42,780
Ages 55 to 59:	23,280
Ages 60 to 64:	12,898
Ages 65 or older:	11,555
Total	816,148

Figure 2.5 A table that contains excessive non-data ink

Patient Age at Diagnosis	Number of AIDS Cases Diagnosed
< 5	6,975
6 to 12	2,099
13 to 19	4,428
20 to 24	28,665
25 to 29	105,060
30 to 34	179,164
35 to 39	182,857
40 to 44	136,145
45 to 49	80,242
50 to 54	42,780
55 to 59	23,280
60 to 64	12,898
65+	11,555
Total	816,148

Figure 2.6 A more efficient table design

Note, too, the light gray reference lines (called "leader lines") that separate groups of data. Although these lines are not, strictly speaking, "data ink," they are valuable because they aid in comprehension.

Eliminating non-data ink is only one way to achieve an efficient graph; you can also improve the data-ink ratio by adding more data. For example, annotation is one of the most useful techniques for increasing a graph's explanatory power and showing readers what the numbers mean. In Figure **2.7**, which graphs the price performance of Apple stock in 2004–2005, annotations highlight events related to the company's iPod device—arguably the key driver of the stock price in that period. Such annotations give the readers a richer sense of how the numbers fit into an overall business context.

Figure 2.7 A graph that uses annotations to highlight and explain data points

Source: Stock prices from Yahoo Finance. http://finance.yahoo.com/q/hp?s=AAPL

Shipment and launch data from Apple Computer, Inc., press releases

Apple Computer, Inc.
Closing Stock Price at Week End
(2/27/04 – 2/18/05)

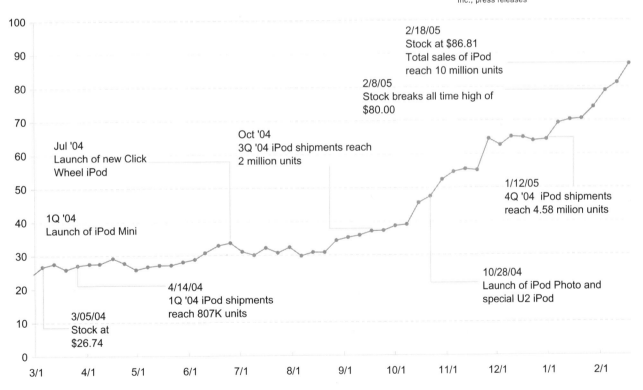

Ensure integrity

The final—and arguably most important—principle to follow in the creation of graphics is integrity. By that we mean not only that the information is true and correct but that it is presented in a way that avoids distorting the truth.

One all too common distortion occurs when graphs are created with selective scaling. The two annual earnings-per-share graphs shown below have the same data (and presumably correct data) but use different scales, which convey entirely different messages. Figure **2.8**, with its minimum starting point at $1.50, suggests much greater variability in earnings, year over year, than Figure **2.9**—and, even worse, a much larger increase in the most recent pair of years plotted (Year 4 to Current Year). By shortening the scale, Figure **2.8** magnifies differences in a misleading way.

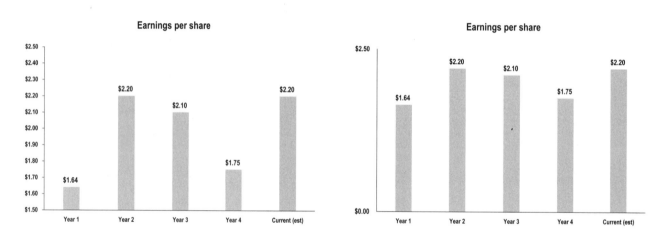

Figure 2.8 The shortened scale on this graph's Y-axis magnifies differences.

Figure 2.9 With its Y-axis scale beginning at zero, this graph provides a more accurate view of the data.

In most cases, graphs should be constructed so that the area representing the data is directly proportional to the quantities that are represented. In Figure **2.8**, the actual spatial difference representing year over year change from Year 4 to the current year amounts to 180%; in contrast, Figure **2.9**, with a $0 to $2.20 scale, represents spatially a difference of 26%—the actual percentage increase in per-share earnings.

Again, Tufte has formulated an interesting metric, the "lie factor" ratio,[3] where:

$$\text{Lie factor} = \frac{\text{size of effect shown in graphic}}{\text{size of effect in the data}}$$

3 Tufte, E. *The Visual Display of Quantitative Information*, 1983, p. 57.

A lie factor that hovers around 1.0 suggests that a graph is not distorting its data. In the case of our improperly scaled earnings per share graph, the lie factor is a whopping 6.92 (1.80/.26).

A second common distortion occurs when graphs are rendered in three dimensions, as in Figure **2.10** below showing market share. Competitor C has a 40% market share, yet in the 3-D pie chart, the area taken up by its slice is much larger. In a two-dimensional rendering, such as Figure **2.11**, the area that represents the data is directly proportional to the quantities represented.

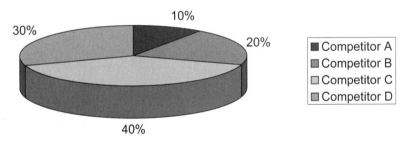

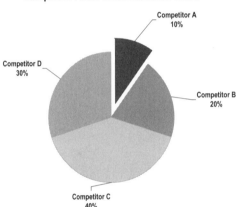

A final note on integrity and the lie factor: in producing some business graphics, you may find yourself tempted to manipulate scale in order to make an important effect visible on the graph. Is this an instance of lying? In these cases, it's useful to employ a variation on the lie factor ratio:

Figure 2.10 (left) A 3-D pie chart magnifies the size of slices at the front of the pie.

Figure 2.11 (right) In a 2-D pie chart, the size of the slice is directly proportional to the data it represents.

$$\text{Lie factor for business graphics} = \frac{\text{size of effect shown in graphic}}{\text{size of the business effect of the data}}$$

If, for example, in a highly competitive business, a 2% increase in market share year over year translates into a 10% difference in revenues and/or profits, a scale that shows a 10% difference may be appropriate.

TABLES

With the advent of word processing and spreadsheet software, making tables has never been easier or more prevalent. Understanding how to organize your data and design your layouts can help your tables be more effective. In this section, we will first look at the structure of tables, then table types, and finally best practices in designing tables.

Table structure

The easiest way to visualize a table is to think of it as a box divided into a number of parts. Figure **2.12** provides a common set of terms for the parts of a table. We will use these terms through the rest of the chapter.

Below are definitions of the terms that may not be self-explanatory:

- The **body** of the table is the rectangular area containing data values; it is the core of the table.

- A **cell** is the intersection of a vertical column and a horizontal row.

- A **footer** is a row that summarizes all the rows in a data table. A **group footer** summarizes a subset of rows.

- A **column header** labels the columns; when a header spans multiple columns, it is called a **spanner header**. In many (but not all) tables, there are **row headers** that label the rows. When a header applies to multiple headers, it is called a **row spanner header** or a **group header**.

- **Rules** are horizontal or vertical lines that are sometimes used to separate header rows from the body of a table or separate data values within a table. **Grids** are a system of intersecting horizontal and vertical rules.

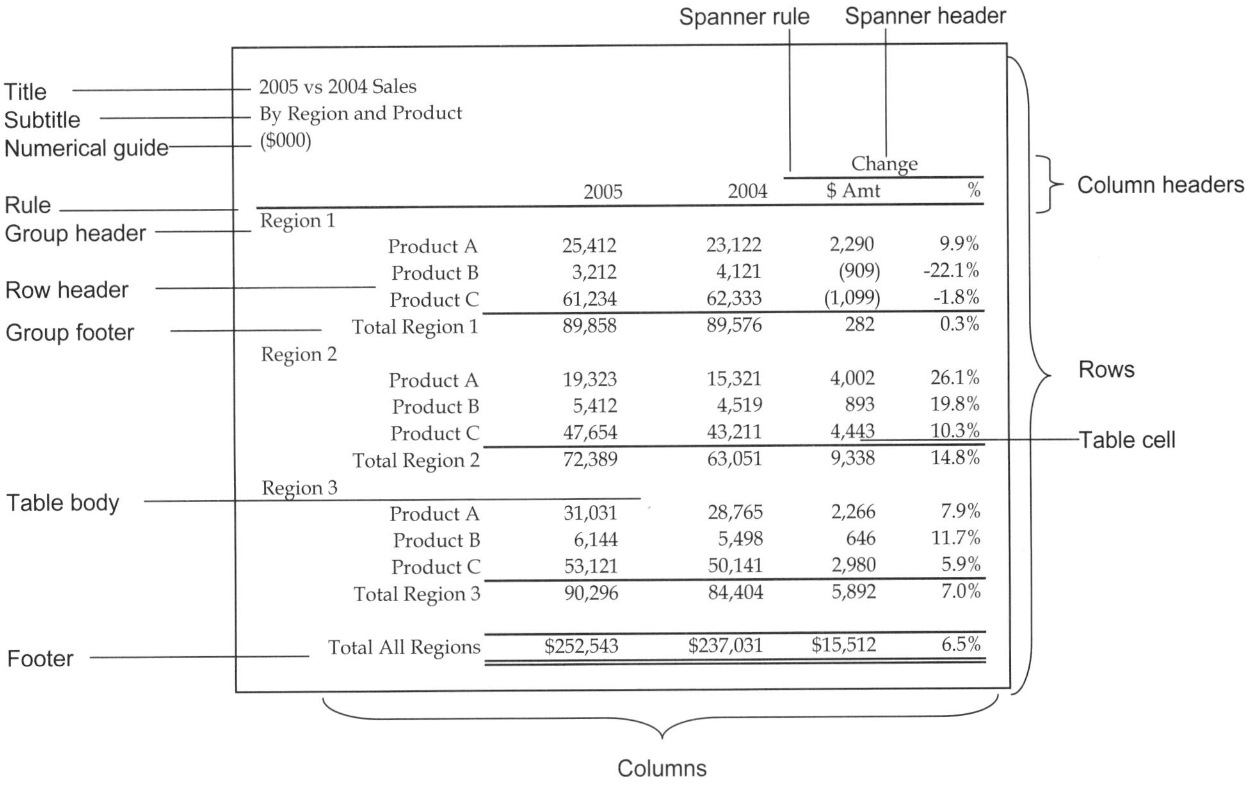
Spanner rule
Spanner header
Title
Subtitle
Numerical guide
Rule
Group header
Row header
Group footer
Table body
Footer
Column headers
Rows
Table cell
Columns

2005 vs 2004 Sales
By Region and Product
($000)

			Change	
	2005	2004	$ Amt	%
Region 1				
Product A	25,412	23,122	2,290	9.9%
Product B	3,212	4,121	(909)	-22.1%
Product C	61,234	62,333	(1,099)	-1.8%
Total Region 1	89,858	89,576	282	0.3%
Region 2				
Product A	19,323	15,321	4,002	26.1%
Product B	5,412	4,519	893	19.8%
Product C	47,654	43,211	4,443	10.3%
Total Region 2	72,389	63,051	9,338	14.8%
Region 3				
Product A	31,031	28,765	2,266	7.9%
Product B	6,144	5,498	646	11.7%
Product C	53,121	50,141	2,980	5.9%
Total Region 3	90,296	84,404	5,892	7.0%
Total All Regions	$252,543	$237,031	$15,512	6.5%

Figure 2.12 A diagram that labels the parts of a table; this is not intended to illustrate best practices in table design.

Table types: reference tables, decision tables, and message tables

When categorized by communication purpose, it is useful to distinguish between three types of tables: reference tables, decision tables, and message tables. **Reference tables** are, as the term implies, meant for reference: they gather up large amounts of data about a particular subject or set of statistics. **Decision tables** are designed to help you make a decision or chose an item or a set of items. Both reference tables and decision tables have a neutral tone. **Message tables**, in contrast, are created to convey a specific message or provide a particular insight into the data; they often extract a subset of data from reference tables to make a particular point.

Reference tables—Typical reference tables include accounting reports such as balance sheets and income statements. Many government statistical tables can be considered reference tables. For example, the U.S. Department of Commerce, through its Bureau of Economic

Analysis, produces a large of number of economic statistics in table form; Figure **2.13**, for example, is a table that shows percentage change in the Gross Domestic Product of the USA.

Percent Change From Preceding Period in Real Gross Domestic Product (Percent)

				Seasonally adjusted at annual rates				
				2005		2006		
	Line	2004	2005	III	IV	I	II	III
Gross domestic product	1	**3.9**	**3.2**	**4.2**	**1.8**	**5.6**	**2.6**	**1.6**
Personal consumption								
expenditures	2	**3.9**	**3.5**	**3.9**	**0.8**	**4.8**	**2.6**	**3.1**
Durable goods	3	6.4	5.5	9.0	−12.3	19.8	−0.1	8.4
Nondurable goods	4	3.6	4.5	3.4	3.9	5.9	1.4	1.6
Services	5	3.5	2.6	3.2	2.0	1.6	3.7	2.8
Gross private domestic								
investment .:...........................	6	**9.8**	**5.4**	**5.2**	**16.2**	**7.8**	**1.0**	**−2.0**
Fixed investment....................	7	7.3	7.5	6.3	2.8	8.2	−1.6	−1.4
Nonresidential	8	5.9	6.8	5.9	5.2	13.7	4.4	8.6
Structures.........................	9	2.2	1.1	−7.0	12.0	8.7	20.3	14.0
Equipment and software	10	7.3	8.9	11.0	2.8	15.6	−1.4	6.4
Residential...........................	11	9.9	8.6	7.1	−0.9	−0.3	−11.1	−17.4
Change in private inventories ...	12	....						
Net exports of goods and								
services	13	....						
Exports	14	9.2	6.8	3.2	9.6	14.0	6.2	6.5
Goods...................................	15	9.0	7.5	3.7	11.5	17.3	6.0	10.0
Services	16	9.7	5.1	2.1	5.5	6.7	6.7	−1.5
Imports	17	10.8	6.1	2.5	13.2	9.1	1.4	7.8
Goods...................................	18	10.9	6.7	2.7	14.1	9.4	−0.1	9.5
Services	19	10.0	2.8	1.2	8.3	7.4	9.9	−1.0
Government consumption								
expenditures and gross								
investment...........................	20	**1.9**	**0.9**	**3.4**	**−1.1**	**4.9**	**0.8**	**2.0**
Federal	21	4.3	1.5	9.6	−4.6	8.8	−4.5	1.7
National defense..................	22	5.9	1.7	11.2	−9.9	8.9	−2.0	−0.7
Nondefense	23	1.2	1.1	6.2	7.1	8.5	−9.3	6.9
State and local.......................	24	0.5	0.5	−0.1	1.0	2.7	4.0	2.1

Figure 2.13 A typical reference table

This table gathers up each percentage change in the USA's Gross Domestic Product, overall and by category, for the years 2004 and 2005. Reading it is straightforward: we know, for instance, that in 2005, the Gross Domestic Product increased 3.2% over 2004. The numbers are presented "as is," without a message. There is no way we can tell by the numbers in the table whether a 3.2% increase in GDP in 2005 is good, bad, or somewhere in between.

Notice, too, that this table is a bidirectional table (sometimes called a matrix). Categories are laid out in both rows and columns. To locate a specific value associated with two categories, you look in the cell where rows and columns intersect.

Other tables are unidirectional: categorical subdivisions are arranged across the columns or down the rows—but not both ways. In Figure **2.14** categorical divisions (regions) are listed down the rows. Sales and Expenses are not categorical subdivisions; they are sets of quantitative values.

Decision tables—Like reference tables, decision tables have no message. Instead, they are designed to guide the reader to make a specific decision based upon reading the elements of the table. Internal Revenue Service tables are typical examples of this table type.

Note how the IRS table in Figure **2.15** provides explicit guidance in the user's decision-making process of calculating taxable income. When you create a decision-making table, you should always strive to make the process of arriving at the proper decision (that is, finding the cell with the proper information) as efficient and explicit as possible.

Sales and Expenses by Region

Region	Sales ($MM)	Expenses ($MM)
East	$1.5	$0.3
West	2.7	0.8
North	3.4	1.0
South	4.4	1.0

Figure 2.14 A unidirectional table with categories (regions) arranged down the rows

Figure 2.15 An Internal Revenue Service table designed to facilitate decision making

If your taxable income is:		The tax is:	of the amount over—
Over—	But not over—		
$0	$7,300	·········· 10%	$0
7,300	29,700	$730.00 + 15%	7,300
29,700	71,950	4,090.00 + 25%	29,700
71,950	150,150	14,652.50 + 28%	71,950
150,150	326,450	36,548.50 + 33%	150,150
326,450	·········	94,727.50 + 35%	326,450

Message tables—In contrast to the more neutral tables we have been reviewing, Figure **2.16** on the following page is a message table. It contains data adapted from information provided by the Freedom House Foundation (a nonpartisan, nonprofit organization that promotes human rights, democracy, free market economics, the rule of law, and independent media). This table is designed to convey long-term trends in the development of democratic institutions in nations around the globe.

Here the information is organized to shape our understanding of trends in democratization worldwide. Note the explicit message in the table title.

Figure 2.16 A table designed to convey a message, which is explicitly stated in the title

Data source: Freedom in the World: 2003, Freedom House, www.freedomhouse.org/research/survey2003.htm, p. 10.

Since 1973, freedom has increased across the globe

Countries by Freedom Category

	1973		1983		1993		2003	
Free	43	28.7%	54	32.7%	75	40.3%	89	46.4%
Partly Free	38	25.3%	47	28.5%	73	39.2%	55	28.6%
Not Free	69	46.0%	64	38.8%	38	20.4%	48	25.0%
Total	150	100.0%	165	100.0%	186	100.0%	192	100.0%

In the past 30 years, not only has the number of countries in the world grown, but the number of free countries has grown also. In *Free* countries, citizens enjoy a high degree of political and civil freedom. *Partly Free* countries are characterized by some restrictions on political rights and civil liberties, often in a context of corruption, weak rule of law, ethnic strife, or civil war. In *Not Free* countries, the political process is tightly controlled and basic freedoms are denied.

Within these categories of tables—reference, decision, and message—you can create tables that contain numbers, text, or a combination of the two. The table illustrated above is a number (that is, data) table. Figure **2.17** is an example of a table that combines text and numbers.

Figure 2.17 A table that organizes text to allow efficient comparison

Source: Adapted from *The New York Times*, November 19, 2004; IMS Health; NDCHealth.

Drug	Serevent	Meridia	Bextra	Accutane	Crestor
Used For	Asthma	Weight loss	Arthritis, pain, and inflammation	Severe acne	A statin, used to lower cholesterol
Entered The Market	1994	1998	2001	1982	2003
Prescriptions In 2003	n.a.	758,000	10,374,000	n.a.	481,000
Sales In 2003	$200 million	$75 million	$936 million	$300 million	$54 million
Concerns	Two studies have suggested that the drug may increase asthma deaths	The drug produces little weight loss but can raise blood pressure	Two studies have linked drug to an increased risk of heart attacks	Prescribed to many young women despite its known risk of birth defects; 1% become pregnant	Can cause muscle damage and kidney failure

Text-oriented tables like this are particularly helpful in presenting comparative information. With this table, it is easy to compare, at a glance, the 2003 sales of the five drugs—as well as the severity of the concerns about their side effects. If this information were written in paragraph form, with one paragraph per drug, sales figures would no longer be adjacent to each other; they would be separated by many lines of text and thus would be difficult to compare.

Best practices in designing tables

Figure **2.18** (on page 34) illustrates key best practices in table design. These apply equally to reference tables, decision tables, and message tables.

Title each table—Give every table you produce a specific title that captures the table's content the way a good newspaper headline captures the essence of its accompanying story. In a reference or decision table, be specific about the kind of information included. In a message table, structure the title to encapsulate the message.

Number tables when you have multiple tables—Properly numbered, tables can be referenced further on in a document, or in new documents.

Eliminate heavy grid lines—Don't imprison your data in a grid of black lines; use simple column headers and spanners to separate data from labels. For some tables, particularly text tables, you may want to use row and column borders, but opt for light gray lines. For large reference tables with many rows of data, use light lines to separate natural groupings of the data.

Minimize shading—Use shading strategically to highlight data or to distinguish alternate rows. Again, try to keep to a minimum the non-data ink in your display. If you opt for shading, use gray; avoid white text on black background.

Use sentence case—All caps are distracting.

Align data and headings effectively—Different kinds of data require different alignments.

> *Align numbers to the right*—Keep decimal points aligned. Use a consistent number of decimal places in all values in a column.

> *Align dates to the left*—Use a date format that maintains a consistent width.

> *Align all other text to the left, with a couple of exceptions*—Exception: If text data all have the same number of characters, you may choose to center that data (see the data columns in Figure **2.18** Table 1a as an example).

> Exception: If row headers exhibit a wide range of widths, you may choose to right align them so that they are each an equal distance from the first value in the body of the table (see the row headers in Figure **2.18** Table 1a as an example).

Align column headers with data—Match the alignment of the data in the column below.

Keep table design consistent—An array of different table designs within a single document will be disorienting to a reader; use identical or highly similar designs throughout.

In Figure **2.18**, you will see these best practices illustrated in a before and after version of two tables that analyze the cost per sales call of a sales forces that serves a number of different markets.

The "Before" design on the top has a host of extraneous elements and is virtually unreadable. The "After" design is much easier to read: it uses good white space and just a few ruled lines that readers can use as reference lines to help locate specific data items.

Figure 2.18 Before and after example of redesigned table

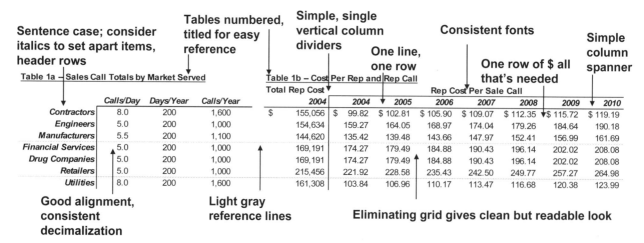

Before

All caps for header rows, items?

Misaligned items

Unnecessary cell padding

Too many $

Inconsistent fonts

Excessive grid lines, column dividers

Table not numbered or titled

MARKET SERVED	SALES CALLS/DAY	# DAYS	TOTAL CALLS
CONTRACTORS	8	200	1,600
ENGINEERS	5	200	1,000
MANUFACTURERS	5.5	200	1,100
FINANCIAL SERVICES	5	200	1,000
DRUG COMPANIES	5	200	1,000
RETAILERS	5	200	1,000
UTILITIES	8	200	1,600

TOTAL REP COST	COST PER SALES CALL							
2004	2005	2005	2006	2007	2008	2009	2010
$ 155,056.00	$ 99.82	$ 102.81	$ 105.90	$ 109.07	$ 112.35	$ 115.72	$ 119.19
$ 154,634.00	$ 159.27	$ 164.05	$ 168.97	$ 174.04	$ 179.26	$ 184.64	$ 190.18
$ 144,620.00	$ 135.42	$ 139.48	$ 143.66	$ 147.97	$ 152.41	$ 156.99	$ 161.69
$ 169,191.00	$ 174.27	$ 179.49	$ 184.88	$ 190.43	$ 196.14	$ 202.02	$ 208.08
$ 169,191.00	$ 174.27	$ 179.49	$ 184.88	$ 190.43	$ 196.14	$ 202.02	$ 208.08
$ 215,456.00	$ 221.92	$ 228.58	$ 235.43	$ 242.50	$ 249.77	$ 257.27	$ 264.98
$ 161,308.00	$ 103.84	$ 106.96	$ 110.17	$ 113.47	$ 116.68	$ 120.38	$ 123.99

After

Sentence case; consider italics to set apart items, header rows

Tables numbered, titled for easy reference

Simple, single vertical column dividers

One line, one row

Consistent fonts

One row of $ all that's needed

Simple column spanner

Table 1a – Sales Call Totals by Market Served

	Calls/Day	Days/Year	Calls/Year
Contractors	8.0	200	1,600
Engineers	5.0	200	1,000
Manufacturers	5.5	200	1,100
Financial Services	5.0	200	1,000
Drug Companies	5.0	200	1,000
Retailers	5.0	200	1,000
Utilities	8.0	200	1,600

Table 1b – Cost Per Rep and Rep Call

Total Rep Cost	Rep Cost Per Sale Call						
2004	2004	2005	2006	2007	2008	2009	2010
$ 155,056	$ 99.82	$ 102.81	$ 105.90	$ 109.07	$ 112.35	$ 115.72	$ 119.19
154,634	159.27	164.05	168.97	174.04	179.26	184.64	190.18
144,620	135.42	139.48	143.66	147.97	152.41	156.99	161.69
169,191	174.27	179.49	184.88	190.43	196.14	202.02	208.08
169,191	174.27	179.49	184.88	190.43	196.14	202.02	208.08
215,456	221.92	228.58	235.43	242.50	249.77	257.27	264.98
161,308	103.84	106.96	110.17	113.47	116.68	120.38	123.99

Good alignment, consistent decimalization

Light gray reference lines

Eliminating grid gives clean but readable look

There are many types of graphs. In his comprehensive illustrated reference book *Information Graphics*, Robert L. Harris has entries for 27 basic graph types (such as line graph, column graph, bar graph, etc.). And within each graph type, there are many variations (for example, Harris catalogues 18 variations on the basic bar graph), all of which are made easier to execute by the availability of hundreds of reasonably priced software products. Although Microsoft Excel has become the de facto graphing program in most businesses, many other specialized graphics programs are also available, particularly software that targets the scientific, engineering, and statistical communities.

With all the choices and options available in graphing, it's easy to be overwhelmed. However, we believe that there is a core set of graphs that serve most business purposes well and a core set of design principles that can help you design elegant graphs, no matter which graph type or variation you wish to execute.

First, we will discuss this core set of graph types. Then we will focus on best practices for designing graphs.

Graph Types

Although there are more than two dozen graph types, most fall into one of the following nine categories enumerated in the Graph Selection Table on the following pages.

- **Pie chart** showing the relative size of parts of one item

- **100% column** comparing identical parts of multiple items

- **Bar chart** comparing multiple items, according to a single characteristic

- **Column chart** displaying changes in one or more items over time, with a few observations

- **Line chart** displaying changes in one or more items over time, with many observations

- **Histogram (step-column)** displaying how groupings fall into a series of progressive ranges

- **Histograph (frequency polygon)** displaying how many items fall into a large-scale distribution pattern

- **Paired bar chart** displaying correlation between two variables with a small data set

- **Scatter plot** displaying correlation between two variables with a large data set

"Sometimes I see graphs that are by themselves, without a story line. The graphs you produce should tell a story."

Jaideep Bajaj
Managing Director
ZS Associates

Purpose

Show parts of one item.

Best graph to use

Pie chart

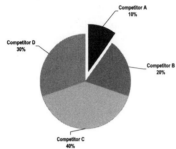

Competitor A has smallest market share

Examples

Show the percentage of:

- market share held by each of the products in a market
- employees at each salary level
- sales for each of the sales regions

Best practices

- Limit to five or fewer segments.
- Label each segment and provide percentage values. Put most significant segment at 12:00.
- If segments are equally significant, arrange from smallest to largest.
- Show emphasis with a darker color or by "exploding" the emphasized segment.

Purpose

Compare parts of multiple items.
-

Best graph to use

100% column

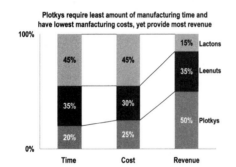

Plotkys require least amount of manufacturing time and have lowest manfacturing costs, yet provide most revenue

Examples

Show how the percentage breakdown differs for:

- cost of product components for multiple versions of that product
- market share of each of a set of products in multiple regions

Best practices

- Use instead of multiple pie charts.
- Put most important component at the bottom of the column so that the most important components share the same baseline.
- To emphasize relationships, use a line to connect series.

Purpose

Compare multiple items, according to a single characteristic.

Best graph to use

Bar chart

Price per pound of key commodities

Examples

Compare:

- prices
- speed
- cost

Best practices

- Add value labels on the bars or at the ends of bars.
- Arrange from largest to smallest if your purpose is to rank items; otherwise, arrange in an order consistent with your message.
- Use color to highlight bars you want to focus on or to group categories of bars.

Purpose	**Best graph to use**	**Examples**	**Best practices**
Show changes over time for a relatively small number of discrete time periods.	Column chart	Compare sales, profits, prices, manufacturing defects over: • a series of years • a series of months • a series of production periods	• Do not use for item comparison; columns imply time. • Make the space between the columns narrower than the width of the columns. • Use color or shading to emphasize one point in time more than others.

Purpose	**Best graph to use**	**Examples**	**Best practices**
Show changes over time to emphasize a trend.	Line chart	Show trends for: • financial data • demographic data • sales data • price data	• Line charts emphasize movements and angles of change; use to emphasize a trend over many time periods. • Provide value labels wherever possible; if too cluttered, present key values.

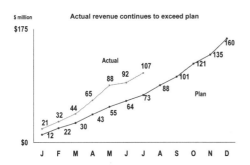

Purpose	**Best graph to use**	**Examples**	**Best practices**
Group data within a series of progressive ranges.	Histogram (step-column)	Show frequency or distribution over: • price ranges • age ranges • date ranges • income ranges	• Generally, use groups (buckets) of equal size, unless unequal groups make better sense. You may want to use a larger bucket at the lower and upper end of the graph, in order to make the graph more concise. • Label the X-axis with range values. • Avoid overlapping range labels such as 0–5, 5–10; instead use 0–4.9, 5–9.9.

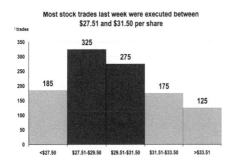

Purpose

Plot the distribution of a continuous series of data to show the pattern of distribution.

Best graph to use

Histograph (frequency polygon)

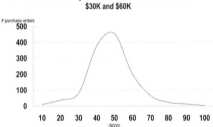

Examples

Explore distribution patterns for such things as:

- annual income per capita worldwide (or annual income of employees in a company)
- days required to ship an order
- manufacturing defects distributed over manufacturing dates

Best practices

- Use a histograph to emphasize the shape and angle of the trend, but only when you have enough measurements to show a trend.
- Do not include range labels on the X-axis. Instead, use discrete measurement point.
- To highlight a specific area of the distribution, use light gray vertical references line or shade the area under the relevant part of the curve.

Purpose

Compare any variables you believe may be related for a small set of discrete items.

Best graph to use

Paired bar

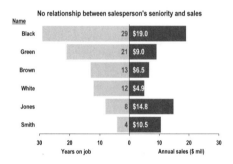

Examples

Explore relationship between:

- pay and performance for a set of sales people
- attendance and grades, for a set of students
- cost and price, for a set of products

Best practices

- Plot the independent variable on the left, in a low-to-high or high-to-low sequence. If variables correlate according to the expected pattern, the paired bars will be mirror images.
- Place labels on the inside base of the bars so that they line up vertically.

Purpose

Compare variables you believe may be related for a large data set.

Best graph to use

Scatter plot

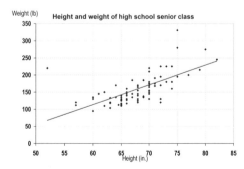

Examples

Explore relationship between:

- price and sales, for a large set of products
- height and weight, for a large set of children
- length of flight versus cost of flight, for a large set of airline routes

Best practices

- Plot the independent variable on the X-axis the dependent variable on the Y.
- If variables correlate, they will cluster around a diagonal line from the lower left of the chart to the upper right.

As with tables, in designing graphs it is important to follow the four basic design principles:

- Design for a purpose.

- Be explicit: show data, label accurately, annotate, highlight, and order.

- Maximize data ink; minimize non–data ink.

- Ensure integrity.

Here are key best practices for implementing these principles in graph design:

Title your graphs—Every graph should have a headline that encapsulates its data, purpose, and/or message. A succinct yet precise headline clarifies the meaning of the graph and allows it to stand alone. Readers will know what the graph means, even if it is reused in different settings. If the graph is plotting data from a specific time frame, it is good practice to indicate the time period in the title (or in a footnote).

Avoid 3-D effects—Three-dimensional effects create distortions in scale and violate the principle of maximizing data ink and minimizing non-data ink. Also, avoid cross hatching and other ink patterns; instead, choose solid colors or good grayscale with differentiation that is easily seen both on the computer screen and the printed page.

Avoid legends whenever possible—Consider using labels instead, placing them as near as possible to the lines or bars. Legends require eye movement back and forth, and thus require additional perceptual effort to match legend colors to the actual data rendered. If you do need to use a legend, be sure distinctions are visible both in color and in grayscale.

Avoid contrasting borders around objects—An additional color as a border is unnecessary if you are graphing only a single data series (with just one color) or you have created a graph with sufficient color differentiation between data items. Borders are also unnecessary—and distracting—around legends and the plot areas of graphs.

Use annotations—Annotations can highlight key data changes or focus on specific data points.

Use minimal grid lines—If possible, don't use them at all. If you must use them, use light gray instead of black.

Use thin lines—The human eye can distinguish lines of 1⁄2 point easily, so minimize ink wherever possible. Use thin axes, bars, and arrows.

Display subtle but visible data point marks—Avoid using data point markers that are more than 2 points larger than your smallest font. These will distract the reader.

Use minimal tick marks—In some instances you can eliminate them.

Label all axes unless it is absolutely clear what is being measured—At times, the title of a graph will make it obvious what units are being graphed on the X- or Y-axes. Most of the time, however, it is crucial to label both what is being measured and the units of measurement (for example, $, $ billion, kilograms, widgets sold).

Position axes labels horizontally—Many software programs default to the vertical position for Y-axis labels, which requires readers to tilt their heads to read. You should reorient those labels so they are positioned horizontally in the manner of normal text on the page. In addition, if at all possible, avoid having X-axis labels oriented at an angle: work toward establishing good abbreviations that allow you to use short, horizontal labels.

Opt for value labels on data points, rather than relying solely on the Y-axis scale, wherever possible—Data labels communicate precise, not estimated, values. If your graph contains too many data labels, delete some to avoid clutter. Retain only the most important data labels—or enough to allow readers to interpret the data. If you use data labels, you can also delete most of the value labels on the Y-axis; minimum and maximum values are usually sufficient.

The before and after graphs in Figures **2.19** and **2.20** illustrate the difference that best practices can make. Following these practices often requires you to reformat your graphs from the standard output generated from the "wizard" function in Microsoft programs (such as Excel or PowerPoint) or other graphing software.

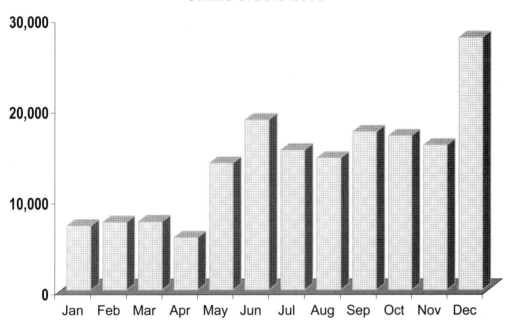

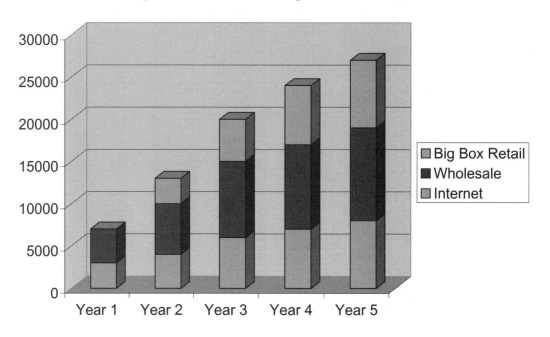

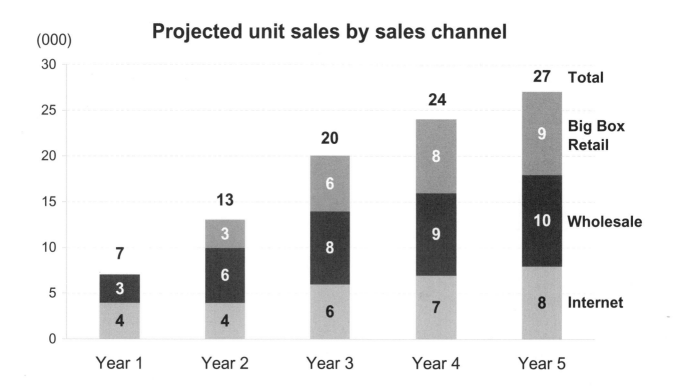

CHAPTER 3 | USING COLOR

Color is one of the most striking elements of visual communication. As readers, we begin processing color messages even before we begin processing text. When we see red text in a user manual, we think stop, danger, warning. Dark blue communicates authority and solidity; green says natural, calm, and cool. When we see a bright, highly saturated color on a subtly-colored graph, we know to pay attention to those specific data points (Figure **3.1**).

Because color has such power, it is important to choose colors carefully in business documents and presentations. It isn't smart to base color decisions on our likes and dislikes. Individual tastes may be idiosyncratic. Likewise, it isn't smart simply to accept the color defaults of our software. Excel's standard purple and gray for bar graphs communicates only one thing: we paid no attention to color.

This chapter provides a framework for choosing colors in a business-like way. It begins by outlining the visual properties of color, establishing a color vocabulary, and discussing how to create a color scheme, also called a palette. Then it offers advice about specific color choice, taking into account the connotations of color, the contexts in which you will use color, and the ability of color to highlight information effectively in both print and projected media. The chapter ends with information about the various systems for specifying color on screen and in print and a list of guidelines to help you choose color.

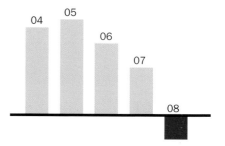

Figure 3.1 Although the bar on the right is the smallest, it grabs our attention most quickly due to its position—and color.

PROPERTIES OF COLOR

As we all learned in high school science, color is the way that our brain interprets different wavelengths of light. Color has three separate properties: hue, value, and saturation. You can use these three properties to specify almost any color and to create a color palette.

Hue

Hue is the word we use to name the colors that we see: red, green, yellow, orange, etc. Different hues have different wavelengths in the color spectrum. In color theory, hues are wrapped around a color wheel in specific relation to each other. Color wheels have evolved over time,

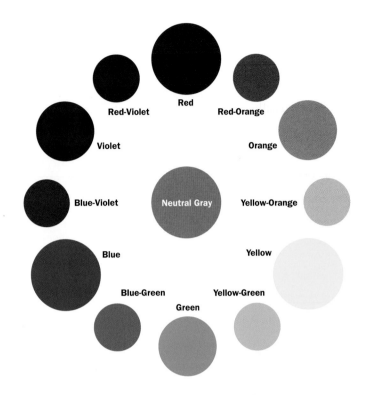

Figure 3.2 This example of a traditional color wheel illustrates the three primary colors (red, blue, and yellow); the three secondary colors (orange, green, and violet); as well as intermediate colors in between. Centrally located, neutral gray is created by a blend of any two complementary colors.

since Sir Isaac Newton developed the first in 1666. Today, the standard wheel we use to combine colors is based on the three primary colors: red, yellow, and blue. In Figure **3.2**, red sits on the top at 0 degrees; yellow is at 120 degrees, and blue is at 240 degrees. The wheel also contains a secondary triad: orange at 60 degrees, green at 180 degrees, and violet at 300 degrees. Other colors are arranged around the wheel in a natural progression between the six major hues. Although there are 360 degrees on a color wheel, we have names for only about 30 hues—a testament to the limitations of our color vocabulary.

The color wheel is our primary tool for creating visually harmonious color palettes based on hues. Hues opposite each other on the wheel are called complementary colors; they have maximum color contrast and often work well together, especially when one is a dominant color and the other is used for accents. Analogous colors are adjacent to each other on the color wheel. They harmonize well with each other. A split complementary color palette uses three colors: a color on the wheel and two colors adjacent to its complement. This combination offers strong contrast but is more subtle than a pure complementary palette. Finally, a triadic color scheme uses three colors spaced evenly around the color wheel. This offers high contrast while retaining harmony.

Value

The second property of colors, value, describes how light or bright the color is; the brighter the color, the higher its value and the more light it emits. Yellow typically has a brighter value than a dark purple. The value of a specific hue can be adjusted by adding more white or black to it. A color with more white in it will look lighter and is often referred to as a "tint" of the color. A color with more black will look darker and is most often referred to as a "shade." For example, adding white to red creates pink; adding black creates maroon (Figure **3.3**). These two colors are the same hue as red, but they have different values.

One way to create an effective monotone color scheme is to combine different values of the same hue (Figure **3.4**).

Saturation

Saturation describes the intensity of a color: how pale or strong it is. If you think about this in terms of ink, saturation describes the amount of pure hue in the ink sample (Figure **3.5**). Saturation is represented as a percentage; the stronger the saturation the closer the color is to a pure hue (100% saturation); the weaker the saturation the closer it is to a neutral gray (0% saturation).[1] It's often effective to use a color palette of low saturation colors, punctuated with a highly saturated, contrasting color to highlight and emphasize key points. Figure **3.6** illustrates two such examples.

CHOOSING SPECIFIC COLORS

While color theory provides guidelines for combining sets of colors into a palette, it does not help us decide what colors to start with. If we want complementary colors, do we choose blue and orange? Red and green? Purple and yellow?

Answering these questions goes well beyond color theory; it leads us to think about what colors mean to people, how colors work in different contexts and media, even how eyesight affects our color perceptions.

The meaning of colors

Colors carry with them a range of psychological, traditional, cultural, and even local meanings that affect people's response to them. Here are some of the traits commonly associated with various colors:

Figure 3.3 In this example, the color at left shows more white than the middle color (red), creating pink; adding black to the middle color creates maroon.

Figure 3.4 This example illustrates two monotone color schemes that exhibit different values of the same hue.

Figure 3.5 This sample shows a highly saturated color at left (magenta) transitioning to a low saturation (neutral gray).

Figure 3.6 In this palette, a highly saturated color (far right) contrasts with two colors that are much less intense.

1 Berryman, G. *Notes on Graphic Design and Visual Communication.* ©1990 by Crisp Publications.

energetic *and* **offensive**

C=0 M=100 Y=100 K=0

friendly *and* **cowardly**

C=0 M=0 Y=100 K=0

intelligent *and* **dull**

C=100 M=50 Y=0 K=0

creative *and* **outrageous**

C=0 M=50 Y=100 K=0

natural *and* **greedy**

C=100 M=0 Y=100 K=0

stylish *and* **moody**

C=50 M=100 Y=0 K=0

Figure 3.7 The traits associated with each color can vary dramatically.

Red

Positive traits: active, ambitious, bold, charismatic, commanding, dramatic, dynamic, energetic, fun, lively, passionate, revolutionary, romantic, sensual, strong, successful, triumphant, vital, warm

Negative traits: aggressive, impatient, offensive, rebellious, violent

Yellow

Positive traits: bright, communicative, creative, expressive, extroverted, friendly, happy, imaginative, innovative, inspiring, intuitive, lively, optimistic, playful, spontaneous, stimulating, youthful

Negative traits: cautious, cowardly, defeated, hazardous, ill

Blue

Positive traits: balanced, calming, clean, conservative, confident, contemplative, dignified, intelligent, logical, loyal, peaceful, protective, rational, reliable, responsible, secure, traditional, trustworthy

Negative traits: cold, depressed, dull, isolated, nostalgic, restrained, sad

Orange

Positive traits: active, changing, cheerful, communicative, creative, earthy, energetic, enthusiastic, exotic, exuberant, friendly, fun, gregarious, humorous, independent, inspiring, stimulating, vibrant, warm

Negative traits: emotional, explosive, outrageous, tiring, wild

Green

Positive traits: adventurous, aspiring, clean, comfortable, conventional, dependable, efficient, fertile, free, fresh, generous, lucky, healthy, natural, prosperous, quiet, relaxed, renewed, reproductive, young

Negative traits: decayed, envious, greedy, ill, inexperienced, naïve

Purple

Positive traits: compassionate, creative, dramatic, dignified, independent, inspirational, intelligent, intuitive, luxurious, magical, majestic, noble, proud, refined, royal, sophisticated, spiritual, stylish, valuable

Negative traits: arrogant, decadent, enigmatic, frail, moody, sad

When you choose a color scheme, it's useful to consider how the meanings of those colors can reinforce your message. Color messages are a key element in corporate branding. Consider two logos (Figure **3.8**) for major oil corporations: Amoco and British Petroleum. The red, white, and blue of Amoco's logo reinforce the message that Amoco—the American Oil Company—is all American.

In 1998, Amoco merged with British Petroleum (BP), and its logo was replaced by the BP helios logo, a green and yellow sunlike image. The BP green and yellow communicate a very different message than the Amoco red, white, and blue. The new colors tell us that oil-based energy is natural and comes from the sun. Instead of speaking to patriotism, it speaks to the public's desire for its energy to be ecological.

Because colors have so many different meanings, it's easy to overlook potentially negative connotations when we make color choices based on our narrow perceptions. Professional graphic designers deal with this challenging situation on a daily basis. Imagine the following situation: Acme Water Corporation, which bottles distilled and spring water, is merging with another water bottling company and wants to redesign its corporate identity to reflect the new, larger organization.

The favorite color of the spouse of Acme's CEO—now the largest share-holder in the combined company—is yellow. Therefore, the Acme CEO wants yellow incorporated into the logo and color palette of the merged firm's corporate identity. At first, this seems a good choice because yellow is understood as a fun, friendly, and warm color.

But now take a moment and consider the connotations that water has when paired with the color yellow. Not good.

Cultural contexts

In addition to their psychological meanings, colors also carry cultural meanings—in different countries and even in different regions within one country. In the United States, black is viewed as a color of serious-ness and sophistication. However, when U.S.-based rental car company Hertz sent out membership materials in black envelopes to Japan, the company did not know that receiving such a missive signifies the death of a close relative. Obviously, this was a poor marketing tactic.[2]

Figure 3.8 When Amoco and British Petroleum (BP) merged in 1998, the patriotic, American red, white, and blue color palette was replaced by yellow and green, colors that reference nature and ecology more directly. (Amoco and BP America logotypes used by permission.)

2 McCarron, C. "Expanding Our Field of Vision Globalization and the Challenging Landscape of Visual Communication," *Communication Arts*. March/April 2003.

The color red in the United States can connote violence, blood, or, in a business context, negative earnings. In other countries, the color red can have different, sometimes positive, connotations. In weddings in India, red garments are used to symbolize love; in Russia red often represents revolution or communism; in China it may represent revolution or, more traditionally, luck and prosperity; the Japanese flag proudly displays a red circle representing the "Land of the Rising Sun"; and in London, red buses and phone booths can be seen on most every street corner. In most Asian cultures, yellow is the royal color and suggests the same cultural associations as purple in the West. In the West, white symbolizes purity and innocence; in Egypt and throughout Islamic North Africa and the Middle East, it symbolizes mourning and death.

Even within one country, cultural associations can affect color perceptions. Marty Fitzpatrick, former Design Director for the National Football League, conducted numerous focus groups on logos and uniforms for NFL expansion teams and new franchises. He found that our perceptions of color are affected by our past associations with them, both individually and collectively.

For example, in almost all cases, he found that the color orange received very low ratings from football fans. In Tennessee, however, orange was overwhelmingly considered the toughest, most appropriate color for a new team. This was not surprising when you consider that the state's main public school and perennial football powerhouse, the University of Tennessee, uses orange as its primary color. Yellow received the lowest ratings of all: people viewed yellow as the least aggressive and weakest color for a football team. However, in a separate survey, when respondents were asked to describe the personality of specific teams, they characterized the Green Bay Packers as strong, tough, and rugged. The Packers' team colors? Yellow and green. The rich history of the Green Bay Packer franchise trumped the idea that men running around in bright yellow pants and helmets would make them less rugged.[3]

3 Interview with the author.

Physical context

Within the range of colors that are appropriate and attractive, you can narrow your color decisions by thinking about the physical context in which the colors will appear. What other colors will be near it? How will the communication be "published": will it be on paper or projected? Will some readers choose to print it in black and white or grayscale?

The surrounding colors

It is nearly impossible to interpret, discuss, or analyze a color by itself. This is because colors are never isolated. You must always consider a color in relation to other colors in the same visual field. For example, if it weren't for London's dark streets and gray stone buildings, the red double-decker buses and the bright red phone booths would not stand out nearly as well. If Japan's rising sun flag were on a blue background instead of stark white, the bright red orb would be far less prominent. Yellow text on a black or dark blue PowerPoint background provides great contrast. If you change the background to white, the text all but disappears.

The relation of surrounding colors is particularly important when you use the colors red and green, which are perceived as very similar—a kind of muddy brown—by the approximately 5% of American males who suffer from red-green color blindness. The bars in Figure **3.9a** may look to a color-blind person like the colors in **3.9b**. The legend, which is color-keyed, will provide no help. If you use colors to distinguish two elements in a graphic, it's best to avoid red and green—or to supplement the colors with effective labeling. The colors in Figure **3.9c**, for example, retain their distinction for a color-blind viewer (**3.9d**).

Print or projection?

Despite the ever-declining cost of color printers, many business documents will still be printed with black ink on white paper. As a result, you always need to print your color graphics in grayscale to see if the rendering of your colors provides sufficient contrast. Your color choices may be both clear and beautiful when output on a color printer—or projected on a screen—but wind up blurring together when you print on a standard black and white printer.

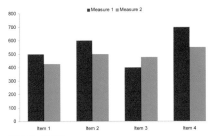

Figure 3.9a

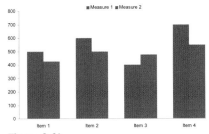

Figure 3.9b

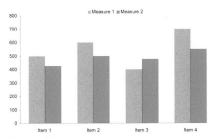

Figure 3.9c

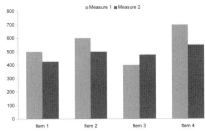

Figure 3.9d

Figure 3.9a–3.9d Red and green (**3.9a**) can be difficult for color-blind viewers to distinguish (**3.9b**). It is wiser to avoid red-green combinations or to choose colors with substantially different values (such as those in **3.9c**) so that their differences are clear even if a viewer cannot distinguish red and green (**3.9d**).

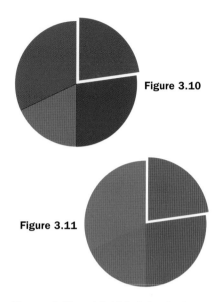

Figure 3.10

Figure 3.11

Figures 3.10 and 3.11 In full color (top), the differences in color of the various slices are clear. But when this chart is converted to grayscale (bottom), it is more difficult to read.

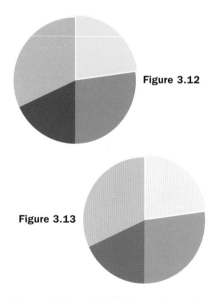

Figure 3.12

Figure 3.13

Figures 3.12 and 3.13 When slices of the pie differ not only in hue but also in value, the color pie chart (top) and its grayscale version (bottom) are equally legible.

For example, the pie chart at left conveys information clearly in full color (Figure **3.10**), but when this same informational graphic is printed in grayscale (Figure **3.11**), it is suddenly much more difficult to read. This often happens due to similarities in value. A redesign of the graphic that considers not just color but also value (Figure **3.12**) clearly illustrates the difference in legibility when it is converted to grayscale (Figure **3.13**).

If you know that your document will be produced in grayscale and you plan to use information that must be distinguished within graphics, try to make the value of the colors (or grays) you choose at least 20% different from each other. If you include white in the group, this allows six value choices: 0%, 20%, 40%, 60%, 80%, and 100%.

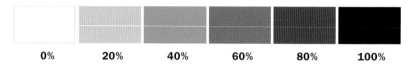

0%   20%   40%   60%   80%   100%

For presentation documents, the color decisions become more complicated. Since many presentations are also printed in black and white, colors still need to be distinguishable in the print version. It's equally important, though, to consider how the colors will look when projected. In a room that is well-lit, a lighter background with darker type will likely be easier to see. In a darker room, a slide with a dark background and lighter type will be equally legible. Contrast is particularly important in projected documents because many projectors wash out the colors—and subtle color distinctions disappear. A dark blue background with red type might look great on your computer monitor; when the presentation is projected, though, the color values may be too similar to allow the red to stand out.

Using color strategically

Many people consider the use of color to be purely aesthetic, but in a business document it should also be strategic and help communicate your message effectively. Consider the different purposes for using color in a document. For example, on graphics you choose colors to:

- **Differentiate data elements**—for example, distinguishing between bars and lines on the same graph.

- **Differentiate data items**—such as distinguishing between two pie slices or two lines.

- **Identify similar data items**—by making them the same color.

- **Differentiate data elements from reference elements**—using different colors for grid lines and axes, as opposed to other data elements.

- **Emphasize different aspects of the data**—for example, in a column chart you may want to have positive columns in one color, negative columns in another.

Color is also useful for prioritizing information and for illuminating points. The reader will be drawn to the most engaging element first, and this is often a strong color. Putting the most important material in the strongest colors will help you control your viewer's response and lead him or her through the page. In a presentation, simple color changes are often enough to illuminate a point. For instance, Figure **3.14** illustrates an excellent way to lead your viewer through a digital presentation by showing the same or similar text on consecutive slides, but changing the color scheme to make the new points stand out.

Symbolizing ideas and concepts is another excellent use of color (e.g., red for danger, green for go or money), but be sure you are not overdoing it. As with too many levels of type, too many colors become more confusing rather than more concise.

SPECIFYING COLORS

Color names are too limited to allow us to specify colors effectively. Although we may know that we would like our color palette to include red, we will still need to identify which red we want to use.

To illustrate this point, it is useful to review color theorist Joseph Albers' seminal book *Interaction of Color*, in which he discusses the limitation of color names:

"If one says 'red' (the name of a color) and there are 50 people listening, it can be expected that there will be 50 reds in their minds. And one can be sure that all these reds will be very different. Even when a

XYZ Research Co. employs this research methodology to survey brand awareness

- Establish purpose of the research
- Design study
- Determine required respondents
- Establish project time line
- Develop survey instrument
- Execute survey
- Present results

XYZ Research Co. employs this research methodology to survey brand awareness

- Establish purpose of the research
- Design study
- Determine required respondents
- Establish project time line
- Develop survey instrument
- Execute survey
- Present results

XYZ Research Co. employs this research methodology to survey brand awareness

- Establish purpose of the research
- Design study
- Determine required respondents
- Establish project time line
- Develop survey instrument
- Execute survey
- Present results

Figure 3.14 In this example, color is used to lead the viewing audience through the steps of a process while still exhibiting all of the individual steps.

Figure 3.15 The RGB color system is used for applications such as computer and television screens.

Figure 3.16 The CMYK color system is used in the printing process.

Figure 3.17 This color can be described in five different ways depending upon the color system you are using:

RGB (Red, Green, Blue):
R=51   G=102   B=153

HSL (Hue, Saturation, Lightness):
H=210° S=67% L=60%

CMYK (Cyan, Magenta, Yellow, Black):
C=86   M=62   Y=21   K=4

Pantone Matching System®: 541 Uncoated

Web safe hexadecimal color: #336699

Color conversion sites on the web or functions in programs like Adobe Photoshop may give you different results.

4 Albers, J. 1975. *Interaction of Color: Revised Edition.* New Haven and London: Yale University Press.

5 www.pantone.com ("Pantone" and "Pantone Matching System" are registered trademarks of Pantone, Inc.)

certain color is specified which all the listeners have seen innumerable times—such as the red of the Coca-Cola signs which is the same red all over the country—they will still think of many different reds."

Albers' example illustrates two "problems" with color. First, Albers tells us, that "our visual memory is very poor, [and] it is hard, if not impossible, to remember distinct colors." Second, it shows that the nomenclature of color is inadequate. "Though there are innumerable colors—shades and tones—in daily vocabulary, there are only about 30 color names."[4]

To combat these limitations, graphic designers have developed several systems for specifying colors. Different systems are used in different contexts and with different media.

- **RGB**—The RGB (Red, Green, Blue) color model (Figure **3.15**) specifies the percentage of red, green, and blue light that create a specific hue. The RGB model is used in many computer applications, including Microsoft Excel and PowerPoint.

- **HSL**—The HSL (Hue, Saturation, Lightness) color model is also used for digital projection; once you have a hue, it allows you to make it lighter or darker—or change its saturation. Microsoft Office applications offer an HSL model for specifying color in addition to the RGB model. (In some applications, HSL is referred to as HSB: hue, saturation, and brightness.)

- **CMYK**—The CMYK (Cyan-Magenta-Yellow-Black) color model is the standard model used in printing for full color documents. It describes all colors as a mixture of the four ink colors cyan, magenta, yellow, and black (Figure **3.16**).

- **Pantone®**—The Pantone Matching System® is the "definitive international reference for selecting, specifying, matching and controlling ink colors."[5]

- **Hexadecimal values**—These six character codes are used to specify colors for websites. There are 216 RGB colors commonly recognized as being "web safe" colors that look the same on all monitors. The hexadecimal ("hex") numbers are translations of the RGB values for these 216 colors.

Many utilities are available on the Internet to translate between different systems of color classification.

GUIDELINES

While there are no hard and fast rules to selecting the "perfect" colors for a business document, we offer the following guidelines as suggestions to make the process easier. For further information regarding the use of color, see the *Annotated Bibliography*.

Be consistent and conservative—Pick a color palette of two or three colors only (Figure **3.18**). Whether using color for a printed document or a digital presentation, develop a system and stick to it. Always remember to err on the side of simplicity. It is easy to get seduced by the ability to use a wide-ranging color palette, but more often than not this will only serve to add visual clutter to your piece. Using regular recurrence of colors for repetitive elements will help you lead your viewer through your document or presentation in a clear and even expected manner.

In choosing a palette, consider the following:

- **Corporate branding**—Ask yourself, "Is this color palette not only the right choice for this document, but is it also appropriate under the larger umbrella of the organization that it represents?" Look to your company's logo for cues and, if possible, see if there is an identity standards manual that you can review.

- **Psychological and cultural meaning of colors**—As discussed previously, different colors mean different things to different people. Know your audience well enough to make appropriate color choices at every step of a project.

- **Surrounding colors**—Individual colors do not operate individually. They affect and are affected by the colors around them. Always consider this phenomenon of relativity.

- **Emphasis**—If you are using color as an emphasis technique, be sure to create a palette that combines less saturated colors with highly saturated colors that can be used for emphasis.

Figure 3.18 Here are some sample color palettes, arranged in groups of three.

R48 G44 B112 C100 M85 Y0 K80	R156 G183 B224 C50 M15 Y0 K0	R84 G158 B66 C80 M10 Y100 K0
R218 G154 B35 C0 M50 Y100 K0	R46 G94 B157 C100 M50 Y100 K10	R229 G219 B126 C0 M5 Y60 K10
R84 G171 B155 C85 M0 Y50 K0	R229 G176 B143 C0 M40 Y40 K0	R113 G27 B37 C35 M100 Y100 K25
R198 G73 B38 C0 M85 Y100 K0	R203 G203 B203 C0 M0 Y0 K25	R54 G44 B114 C100 M90 Y15 K5
R54 G44 B114 C100 M90 Y15 K5	R224 G220 B159 C0 M0 Y40 K15	R93 G126 B188 C80 M40 Y0 K0
R213 G127 B130 C20 M0 Y65 K0	R211 G184 B39 C10 M30 Y100 K0	R148 G64 B40 C20 M85 Y100 K15
R221 G231 B96 C15 M0 Y80 K0	R84 G158 B66 C80 M10 Y100 K0	R87 G0 B80 C45 M100 Y0 K40
R195 G209 B235 C30 M10 Y0 K0	R31 G66 B103 C100 M35 Y0 K55	R178 G116 B45 C20 M65 Y100 K0
R203 G203 B203 C0 M0 Y0 K25	R193 G73 B38 C0 M85 Y100 K0	R67 G58 B53 C0 M25 Y20 K80
R36 G73 B44 C100 M50 Y100 K35	R195 G183 B106 C0 M10 Y60 K25	R111 G111 B111 C0 M0 Y0 K65

Tools to Select Palettes

Color Schemer On-Line

http://www.colorschemer.com/
online.html

Traumwind Color Match

http://traumwind.de/blog/
trw_colormatch.html

Color Scheme Generator

http://wellstyled.com/tools/
colorscheme2/index-en.html

Easy RGB

http://www.easyrgb.com/
harmonies.php#Result

• **The need to print in black and white**—If your document will be printed in limited color or black and white only, choose variations of your colors with different value and saturation so that their grayscale equivalents will look different.

Seek consultation—If you have no talent at picking colors, pick the brain of a graphic designer. For information on selecting a graphic designer, see Chapter 7. Alternatively, you can use one of the color tools available on the web. For example, *Color Schemer On-Line* starts with a single color as the base for a palette, and then provides a set of 16 complementary colors across the spectrum; you can also lighten the scheme into a more pastel range, or darken it to get more primary colors. *Traumwind Color Match* is designed to select a set of six complementary colors, typically for websites, based on entering a hexadecimal number. *Color Scheme Generator* is a sophisticated palette creation tool that applies color wheel concepts to palette selection. With *Easy RGB* you input a base color's RGB numbers (Red, Green, Blue) and a set of complementary colors is presented.

CHAPTER 4 | USING PHOTOS AND ILLUSTRATIONS

The vast majority of day-to-day business communications do not call for accompanying imagery. However, incorporating photos or illustrations in reports, manuals, and presentations can bring greater understanding to the viewer and clarify the meaning of the message. You will need to choose these images wisely; if images are not consistent with the tone and purpose of your communication, they can create confusion and even derail your message. This chapter offers advice about when and how to use images, both photographic and illustrative, to enhance your message and your communication.

USING PHOTOGRAPHIC IMAGES

Both photographs and illustrations tend to speak to the audience more quickly than the written word and offer more immediate emotional value to the viewer. If you are projecting a presentation or sharing a printed document, your viewer's attention will almost always connect to the image first. An excellent example of this is the photo in Figure **4.1**. There is a vast difference between describing something—in this case, a target audience—and showing it. Seeing this group of hip, young, urban professionals raises your level of understanding more quickly than a bullet point list would have, no matter how detailed the language: hip, young, urban, professional, multicultural, fashionable, middle- to high-income, etc. The photograph offers facial expressions, clothing choices, and hairstyles, as well as a setting within which this group "operates."

A photograph also conveys feelings that black letters on a white page simply cannot and so controls the tone of the communication. Looking at our group again, you will see that they appear friendly and outgoing, not serious and introverted. These are specific emotional qualities that the image can capture and express with much more immediacy than text can.

Figure 4.1 A picture can indeed be worth a thousand words: this photograph quickly conveys information that would otherwise take paragraphs of text to describe.

A photograph not only conveys feelings, it can also influence your audience's feelings. A portrait that accompanies the opening letter in an annual report connects the viewer directly to the CEO; showing the breathtaking view of a conference location may entice members to attend the event; a detail image of a product in use will help the audience understand and appreciate the product's clear benefit.

Furthermore, photographs provide a level of authenticity that the written word may not and that illustrations often cannot. Our perception, whether it is fully accurate or not, is that photographs report or document an actual event, a moment in time. They portray a knowable situation.

Color versus black and white photography

Once you've decided that photography is the best way to share information, you'll also need to decide whether to use full color photography or black and white images. There are benefits and drawbacks to each.

A color photograph adds vibrancy to the page or slide. It will no doubt capture the viewer's eye immediately. Color can add to the mood of the information that is being presented. But always be careful not to make the photograph too dominant. A picture that distracts the viewer from other information may negate the whole reason for its existence. Look at the color image of the group in Figure **4.1**. Note how dominant the yellow shirt is. Is it too much? Does your eye focus on the bright color and get pushed away from other details that add information, such as the sparse setting? This happens because color is almost always relative, as discussed in Chapter 3. The yellow's vibrancy has as much to do with the colors around it—the colors that relate to it visually—as it does with the yellow itself.

In this case, a black and white or limited color photograph may be a better choice. Here, the color palette is controlled. The image is just black, white—and perhaps one additional color—along with shades of gray. Figure **4.2**, called a halftone, utilizes one color ink (black) and the paper on which the book is printed. Figure **4.3**, called a duotone, adds a second color, in this case cyan. Depending on the subject matter,

Figure 4.2 Halftone photographs are printed with only one ink color. In the sample above, the image is created using black ink.

Figure 4.3 Duotone photographs are printed with two ink colors. In this sample, the image is created using black and cyan inks.

black and white photography often can have a more immediate quality, even a photo-journalistic feel. Black and white photography, if done well, can also lend an air of sophistication to a piece.

Focusing your viewer

If you find it necessary to photograph a small object or product, take care to highlight the product itself and not the various surrounding elements. As Figure **4.4** illustrates, it is easy for the subject matter to get lost in the clutter. Photographing the object at close range or even on a blank background (known as a "sweep") will eliminate unnecessary peripheral distractions. Most software programs with photo manipulation ability will allow the user to outline the object, thus removing any competing visuals from the image (as in Figure **4.5**).

Figure 4.4 The laptop in the above photograph begins to get lost in the clutter.

Judging a photograph's quality

There are countless books dedicated to analyzing the quality of photographs, and this book will not attempt to cover information that is so easily accessible. However, it is worth mentioning a few key points to consider when you are viewing a photograph that will be incorporated into a business document. If you are sure that the subject matter is appropriate and will add value to the communication, consider the following carefully:

- **Scale**—how big or small does the photo need to be to convey its message appropriately and accurately?

- **Cropping**—how is the subject matter of the photograph included within the frame of the image?

- **Focus**—is the subject matter clear enough for the viewer to access the information?

- **Tonal range**—do the values of the image allow for appropriate visual legibility?

Figure 4.5 In this image, the surrounding clutter is removed, thus focusing the viewer's attention on the computer.

All the above suggestions are meant to ensure that the viewer will notice the image because it brings communicative power to the message and not because it is a bad photo!

Accessing photographic images

Like so much other data and information, photographs are highly accessible over the Internet, which offers a seemingly infinite number of photo resources and makes it easy to browse and purchase photos online. Additionally, as the cost of digital cameras continues to decrease, adding photographic images to your presentation or document becomes simpler all the time.

You can purchase stock photography (and illustrations) online from any number of sites. Simply typing "stock photography" into a search engine will quickly provide access to millions of images. Each online stock agency has various ways to search for the imagery you need; spending just a few minutes browsing these websites will help you understand how to access the pictures. Prices will vary widely, from just a few dollars to a few hundred dollars. And different organizations will have different usage rights. For instance, you may have to pay more for an image that will be used nationally than one that only a few dozen people will view. But paying a few extra dollars for the right photograph will benefit your communication in the long run—and the short run as well.

If a more customized image is necessary for your message—and you believe the photograph can be satisfactorily produced in a fairly short time—consider having the image shot for you. Digital imaging has sped up the photographic process so dramatically that once a photo is taken it can be transferred to an electronic file in a matter of minutes, and often just seconds. However, there is far more to getting a great photo than just pointing the camera and pushing the button—regardless of what the camera companies would have you believe. Subject matter, lighting, cropping, and setting all play an important role in the final picture. When in doubt, consult a professional photographer for help. A bad photograph can often do more harm than good.

Challenges represented by the use of photographs

Despite their communicative power, photographs present a number of challenges. One drawback may be the rate at which the photo begins to look dated. Imagine our group of young professionals (Figure **4.1**) in five years. Will their hairstyles still look good? Will their clothing seem

---

Online stock photography

Searching for "stock photography" online will result in thousands of results. Here are a few such web-based agencies:

www.**alamy**.com

www.**comstock**.com

www.**corbisimages**.com

www.**creatas**.com

www.**gettyimages**.com

www.**inmagine**.com

www.**masterfile**.com

www.**onrequestimages**.com

www.**photos**.com

www.**picturequest**.com

www.**punchstock**.com

www.**rubberball**.com

www.**shutterstock**.com

www.**stockphoto**.com

www.**superstock**.com

www.**veer**.com

www.**wonderfile**.com

appropriately "cool"? And what about ten years from now? Will a four-button suit still be in style? You need to be particularly careful about the photographic representation of technology. An image of someone using the latest and greatest mp3 player or PDA, for instance, will certainly look dated within just a few years' time.

Finally, remember that just because you *can* add images to your presentation or document does not mean you *should*. Like all things, too many photos can muddle the communication. So pick your spots wisely and insert only photographs that support your message.

USING ILLUSTRATIONS

Too many people view illustration as a second choice when photography does not work well. This is not the best way to address your communication problem. Illustrations, photographs, words, charts, maps, and graphs—all should be considered equal arrows in your quiver. It is up to you to identify the best choice to hit your target most accurately. So the questions to ask are, "What idea am I trying to communicate visually, and what is the best way to do so?" There will be projects that you believe from the outset are particularly well suited for illustrations. While photographs do a fabulous job showing people, places, and things, illustrations often represent *concepts* in a far superior way. For instance, a computer-generated axonometric (three-dimensional) view of a production facility can show how a space is best utilized; a perspective drawing of an as-yet-to-be-completed product can illustrate the near future (Figure **4.6**); a painting of a giant pencil bridging a deep chasm can express an intellectual connection between two differing areas.

One example of illustration being superior to photography can be found in instructional manuals. In fact, part of the great success of home furnishings company IKEA can be seen in the assembly instructions that accompany their products. If these instructional illustrations were photographs, the viewer would be overly aware of extraneous elements that hinder the necessary communication. Figure **4.7** is an example of an IKEA illustration that demonstrates the assembly of a drawer. The line drawing makes the connecting mechanism the focal point.

Figure 4.6 A digital rendering of a future product can help to illustrate what it will look like and how it will function. Here, the parts of a simple water pump are shown in an "exploded view."

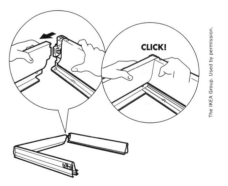

Figures 4.7 In this instructional illustration from IKEA, the simple line drawing includes no unnecessary information, thereby focusing the viewer's attention.

Another excellent example of controlled and appropriate illustrations used in the business world can be found in *The Wall Street Journal.* The front page of each issue incorporates a line drawing of a CEO, politician, or even a Hollywood movie star. Figure **4.8** provides examples of this type of illustration. These simple drawings are handled the same way each time to provide consistency from one day to the next. The limited color (black only), the regular line weight, the deletion of any background, and the consistent scale all control the "feel" of these images so that they appropriately fit with *The Wall Street Journal*'s identity. Just imagine the difference if the newspaper used various uncropped, unedited photographs on the front page each day—as most newspapers do. The variations would undermine the controlled look and feel that *The Journal* has worked so hard to maintain.

Illustrations by John Chui

Figure 4.8 The formal qualities of these portraits hold them together as a group. These include the color, line weight, lack of background, and scale.

Black and white line drawings are only one example of illustration techniques. There are as many styles of illustration as there are styles of photography or writing. So your first challenge is to identify the correct style or tone that the image needs to take: Realistic? Humorous? Horrific? Clever? Whimsical? Whatever tone you choose, be sure it is true to the message. For instance, avoid a cartoon feel in any serious business communication.

Speaking of cartoonlike illustrations, programs like Microsoft Word and PowerPoint offer hundreds of copyright free images. We recommend that you avoid these images. Much of this clip art has a cartoon feel and is overly clichéd. Images like a globe, a heart, and two hands shaking have been used so many times that they don't bring any added value to the communication. Try to be as specific to your content as possible, and make sure that the communicative value of the image justifies the amount of space it requires.

You should also be wary of imagery that stereotypes. If you haven't thought carefully about an image that is available to you at no cost, and you simply use it because it is easily accessible, make sure that it accurately portrays what you want and that it doesn't create cultural, gender, racial, or religious bias. If a free illustration creates ill will with your audience, it may prove more costly than paying for a better one.

Similar to the photographic stock sources mentioned earlier, stock illustrations can be researched, selected, and purchased online. All of the above rules apply, however. If time and budget allow, illustrations can be created for your presentation. As with hiring a photographer, this option is ideal because the end product can be exactly what you want.

Custom illustrations are particularly useful to make the hypothetical come to life. It could be difficult to describe how the pump in Figure **4.6** operates in water. Showing a customized digital illustration of the pump in action (Figure **4.9**) communicates the information quickly.

Figures 4.9 and 4.10 Two hypothetical situations illuminated by illustrations: a digital rendering of a proposed water pump in use (above) and a photo illustration of a proposed building drawn into the existing site photograph (below).

A customized photo illustration—a photo that has been manipulated to include additional elements—is another powerful means to help people conceptualize the hypothetical. Architectural firms use this to great advantage to show what a building will look like in its environment once it is constructed (Figure **4.10**). Although there are many other uses for this kind of imagery, most photo illustrations solve the problem of trying to show the possible change as if it were actual.

Finally, be careful not to mix and match too many styles of illustrations and photographs. Throwing together stylistically unrelated imagery almost certainly will have the effect of making your presentation or paper look amateurish. For example, if small, high-contrast black and white illustrations work best, then stick to that style throughout. If large, full color photographs are necessary, then by all means use them. But use them judiciously, and avoid adding other elements that "look cool" but only serve to clutter the page—and the communication.

PRACTICAL AND TECHNICAL CONSIDERATIONS

As you assemble your business documents, practical considerations will play a key role in the images you select. The first issue will likely be accessibility, but it isn't the only one. For instance, you will need to consider printing costs if you want to create multiple reports. This consideration may lead you to the use of black and white illustrations instead of color. If your readers will access your document digitally, remember that smaller images download faster. So pay careful attention to the size of the electronic files you use.

A good guideline to follow when adding imagery to your document is to understand what form the final product will take. If you plan to give a digital presentation, for instance, there is no reason to have high-resolution images in your electronic file. On the other hand, you may need these larger image files if you plan to print the document later so that the pictures don't become pixelated (Figure **4.11**).

Preparing image files

When you prepare image files to include in documents, you should consider three issues: color format, resolution, and cropping.

Color format—Monitors and projectors operate in the RGB format (Red, Green, Blue), so files for a projected presentation should be saved in this manner. Printers operate on the CMYK system; that is, ink colors of cyan, magenta, yellow, and black. Files being printed by offset printers require colors to be specified in CMYK format.

Resolution—Images with resolution as low as 72 dots per inch, or dpi, will be sufficient for viewing on a computer or projector screen. Even with this low resolution they will still remain sharp. However, if you plan to print your document—whether digitally at your office or at a copy shop (no liquid ink) or at a commercial printer (liquid ink)—the resolution of the picture files you supply must be significantly higher. For instance, most printers (digital and offset) can print up to 300 dpi, a resolution more than four times that of the projected digital file. As you may know, these "high-resolution" images take up much more disk space and download significantly more slowly. This is one reason it is critically important to know how best to crop, save, and place your images.

Pixel

Short for "picture element," a pixel is defined as the basic unit of the composition for an image on a computer monitor or television screen. They are the small, square building blocks that are used to create a picture.

Figure 4.11 If the resolution of an image is too low, the viewer will begin to see the pixels (small squares) that make up the digital file. This also happens when the scale of an image is too drastically increased within an electronic document.

Cropping—Whether you are placing your image file in a document to be projected or printed, you should incorporate only the digital information that you need: no more and no less. As an example, consider again the group photograph in Figure **4.12**. If you need to include only a portion of the entire image, crop the image in its native program to include only the area that you need. If you bring the entire image into your word processing or presentation program and crop it there, it is likely that the file will continue to include the entire image even though you are showing only part of it. This bloats the size of the document file. Multiply this by multiple images and you can see how a document's size can quickly become unmanageable. If you crop the image to exactly what you wish to show, as illustrated in Figure **4.12**, you will decrease the overall file size significantly.

Figure 4.12 If you need to include only part of an image in your document...

...delete all the unnecessary digital information (ghosted at top).

Cropping unnecessary information before you place images in your document can dramatically decrease the size of the entire file.

A word of caution: once you have saved an image file to the appropriate size, do not enlarge the image by more than 10 or 15% when you place it into a document. If you do, you will notice an obvious loss in picture quality. It will begin to look pixelated.

BEST PRACTICES FOR USING IMAGES

- Decide whether or not an image will improve your message.

- Judiciously select the appropriate places in your presentation or document to incorporate your image.

- Decide whether a photograph or an illustration is better suited for the communication.

- Decide what tone the image(s) should project.

- Spend the appropriate time researching and selecting the images.

- Review your selections for quality and consistency. Ask yourself, "Is this image doing what it needs to do?" Also ask yourself whether the combination of images in your document works well or makes the document look disjointed.

- Prepare the files properly for inclusion in the document.

CHAPTER 5 | **INTEGRATING GRAPHICS AND TEXT**

While a picture may be worth a thousand words, in business communication visual elements rarely exist alone without accompanying text. In brochures, on websites, in reports or presentations, pictures go hand-in-hand with words. This short chapter discusses three different roles that visuals play in text—and best practices for integrating the text and visuals.

VISUALS THAT EVOKE FEELINGS

In some cases, visuals need no textual explanation. Consider, for example, the annual report for a pharmaceutical company, which includes pictures of active, healthy people. The report is likely never to refer to these pictures explicitly. Instead, the role of the visual is to *evoke a feeling* in the reader. The picture implicitly says this company is committed to good health. That same report may also include an image of a molecule that the company is researching; this image says the company is rigorous and science based. Visuals designed to influence feelings frequently appear in corporate communications, including brochures, websites, and sales presentations.

VISUALS THAT SUPPLEMENT THE TEXT

In business reports, articles, and white papers, by contrast, visual images typically play other roles and are integrated more closely with text.

Frequently, visuals are intended to *supplement the text*, by supporting a point the text is making. This is the approach taken by most data graphics. While the graph presents the data, the text must contextualize and interpret the data, telling readers what they are looking at (that is, what the information is and where it comes from) and then providing generalizations that highlight the key point the reader should see in the data.

Consider the graph in Figure **5.1**, and compare two versions of text that might accompany it in a business document.

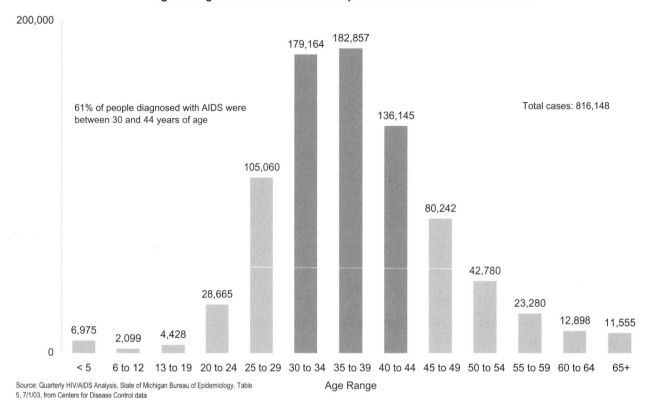

Age at diagnosis of all AIDS cases reported in the U.S. from 1981 to 2001

61% of people diagnosed with AIDS were between 30 and 44 years of age

Total cases: 816,148

Source: Quarterly HIV/AIDS Analysis, State of Michigan Bureau of Epidemiology, Table 5, 7/1/03, from Centers for Disease Control data

Age Range

Figure 5.1 A graph that requires text to elucidate main points

Version A

As Figure **5.1** illustrates, between 1981 and 2001, almost 500,000 people in their 30s to mid-40s were diagnosed with AIDS. By contrast, only 11,555 people 65 years or older were diagnosed.

Version B

We recommend that AIDS prevention efforts be targeted to people in their 20s and 30s. According to data from the Centers for Disease Control (Figure **5.1**), between 1981 and 2001, more than 61% of people who were diagnosed with AIDS were between 30 and 44 years old. Since the mean incubation period for AIDS in adults is approximately 9 years,* it is likely that most of these AIDS patients contracted the disease in their 20s and early 30s. By targeting our efforts at this age group, we will make the most impact.

*Kolata, G. AIDS incubation time often exceeds 9 years. *New York Times*, March 16, 1989.

Version A simply repeats data that can be seen in the graph itself. Version B, by contrast, generalizes from the data and identifies significant patterns. It also integrates the data into an argument.

VISUALS THAT COMPLEMENT THE TEXT

In many documents—especially instructional documents and manuals—visuals are intended to *complement the text*. In other words, the text and the image include different content, both working together to communicate the main idea. Figure **5.2**, for example, offers an illustration of the conceptual design for a finger trainer, a device intended to help stroke survivors regain strength and control over individual fingers. The illustration does an excellent job of showing what the device looks like; explaining this in prose would be cumbersome and ineffective.

But the picture is not sufficient to explain how the device works. This requires complementary prose:

> Figure **5.2** illustrates the design of the finger trainer. The user places his or her wrist in the padded wrist support and slips individual fingers into the loops on the keys.
>
> When training the left hand, the user places the thumb on Key 1 and the fingers on Keys 2 through 5. For the right hand, the thumb goes on Key 6. To train the fingers, the user simply presses down on the keys; a set of wheels and ceramic brakes inside the box provide adjustable resistance. Users can keep track of their progress by means of the LCD feedback display.

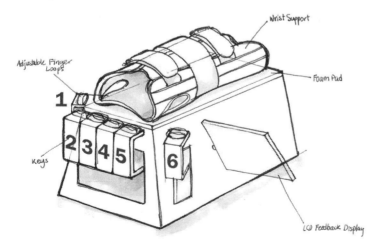

Figure 5.2 Conceptual design for a finger trainer: a device that helps stroke survivors regain individuation in their fingers

(Product designers: Nicholas Graham, Thomas Perez, and Josephine Yang. Graphic designer: Josephine Yang.)

BEST PRACTICES FOR INTEGRATING TEXT AND GRAPHICS

To integrate verbal and visual elements of a text, follow these steps.

- **Refer the reader to the graphic within the text.** Label and number each figure in a document and refer to the graphic by figure number.

- **Place the graphic as close as possible after the first reference.** Do not place graphics before they are mentioned in the text; this will confuse readers.

- **For supplementary visuals, tell the reader what to notice in the graphic.** In a data graphic, what are the important findings or trends? In a picture or illustration, where should we focus our attention? In a diagram, how should we be reading the illustrated relationships?

- **For complementary visuals, provide cues in the text about when and how your readers should use the visuals.** In addition, provide adequate labeling so that you are able to talk about the graphic within your text.

- **Be sure that you have designed the graphic to support the message in the text.** Ask yourself if readers will be able to see what you want them to see.

- **Finally, although the text and graphics are interdependent, design the graphic to be self-explanatory.** Provide enough labeling on the graphic and enough description in the figure name and caption so that readers can understand what they are seeing without reading any accompanying text. This allows readers to scan the document and derive a good deal of information by looking solely at graphics.

CHAPTER 6 | **USING POWERPOINT**

Originally, PowerPoint was designed to replace 35mm slides projected on a carousel projector. Today, in most organizations, PowerPoint is the de facto program for business presentations. It is also increasingly used for business reporting because business readers under time pressure have little tolerance for lengthy reports or memos. PowerPoint requires an author to be succinct and to the point.

PowerPoint dominates business communication for other reasons also: the program is relatively easy to use; a PowerPoint document can be stored and transmitted electronically; it can be projected easily to groups of almost any size, yet printed in hardcopy on any standard laser printer; and it constitutes a basic record of any talk or presentation. In fact, in many organizations, a set of PowerPoint slides may be the only written record of a business decision or issue.

But the program's strengths can also be its weaknesses. Many commentators and experts have bemoaned the use of cryptic bullet point lists, text-heavy paragraphs, meaningless clip art, and data graphics that are impossible to decipher.[1] Although PowerPoint may be *easy to use*, it is *challenging to use well*.

To get the full benefit of the program, a communicator needs to apply principles of good visual communication. A PowerPoint presentation reaches its full potential only when it captures and focuses audience attention, communicates information at a glance, and uses visual techniques to help the audience follow its logic and argument.

In this chapter, we'll address important design principles for taking advantage of PowerPoint as a visual medium. Once you learn these basic principles, you can apply them to any presentation with positive results.

This chapter addresses the following topics:

- Creating an effective template

- Designing coherent and readable slides

- Signaling the presentation flow

"We use Microsoft PowerPoint for just about everything. It's remarkable how often I see it, even just for basic information we might share internally. It's become a 'go-to' software package that almost everyone feels comfortable using. We use it with employees, customers, the news media, with investment analysts, and more."

John Spelich
Vice President
Corporate Communications
Gateway, Inc.

[1] The most widely cited attack against PowerPoint is that by Edward Tufte (2001) in his monograph, *The Cognitive Style of PowerPoint*.

CREATING A TEMPLATE

With the vast proliferation of PowerPoint templates, both supplied by Microsoft and available from other sources, PowerPoint users are overwhelmed by design choices. Many business communicators therefore opt for one of the readily available templates, which often include borders, pictures, and background color gradations. While it may seem that these decorative elements offer "visual interest," they become distracting in a long presentation and often clash with graphics in the slide content.

In business communication, the PowerPoint slide design you choose should always be subservient to your business message. The best approach is to keep your slide design simple and unadorned so your readers can concentrate on the content you are trying to convey.

Fortunately, PowerPoint allows you to create your own slide templates (saved in the Microsoft Template folder as a .pot file). Here are fundamental design guidelines to help you structure a template that supports effective visual communication.

Design your template on master slides

This is the best way to enforce consistency in your visual elements: colors, fonts and font sizes, bullets, headers, footers, and margins will remain consistent from slide to slide. Figure **6.1** illustrates how you might set up elements on master slides.

Figure 6.1a–b The best way to create visual consistency in PowerPoint is to design or choose a template that includes key visual elements on master slides. This figure illustrates elements that you can control through slide masters. These elements are then applied to every slide in the presentation. You can access the master slides from PowerPoint's *View* menu.

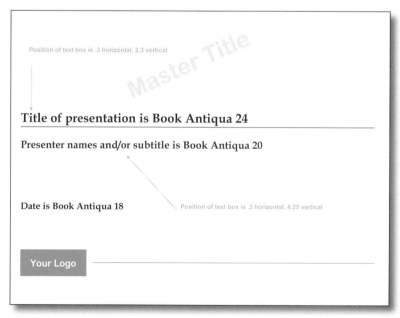

Figure 6.1a Master title

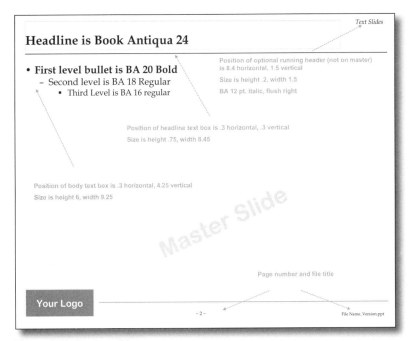

Figure 6.1b Master slide

Use a simple look

Avoid templates with decorative, nonfunctional graphics, like the template in Figure **6.2**. These templates are so overused that they immediately communicate a lack of originality. In addition, the graphic elements on these slides often take up a good deal of space that can be better used for content relevant to your message. If you want to include a thematic graphic that relates to your presentation content, put it on the title slide. Body slides work best when they are relatively plain and have sufficient space for message content, including content-specific graphics. If you would like a logo or other corporate identity item on each slide, put it in the footer where it will be visible but subordinate to the message.

Use basic, solid backgrounds

Use a single, cool color for presentations to be projected in a darkened room; for presentations in a well-lit room (or presentations intended to be read on the computer or in printout form), use a white or light background. Avoid color gradations or fill effects on backgrounds; as Figure **6.3** illustrates, these will often conflict with the color of the font you choose—at least on part of the screen.

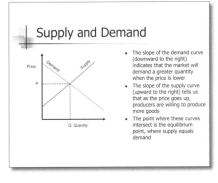

Figure 6.2 Avoid PowerPoint's standard templates that are hackneyed and contain extraneous graphics that don't complement the message on a slide.

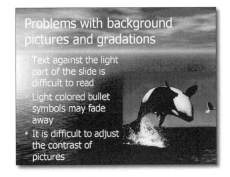

Figure 6.3 Avoid PowerPoint templates with picture or graded backgrounds, which do not provide consistent contrast for the text on the slide.

Use a contrasting color for headlines and text

If you are planning to project with a projector, test your color combination to make sure that the colors contrast sufficiently in that medium.

Use simple bullets

Opt for bullets like this • and avoid overly ornate dingbats and arrows such as ⇨. They take attention away from your content.

Employ a coherent set of fonts

Figure **6.4** on the next page illustrates typical approaches to applying typefaces in PowerPoint. Most often, presentations use a single, legible font like Book Antiqua, Georgia, or Verdana, along with variations in its style such as italic and bold. However, you can also combine fonts within one family such as the Franklin Gothic family (Franklin Gothic, Franklin Gothic Demi and Franklin Gothic Heavy) or the Arial family (Arial Regular, Arial Black, and Arial Narrow).

If you use fonts that are outside the standard set included in Microsoft Windows, be sure to save your file with the fonts embedded. This will allow you to project your file on any other Windows-based computer (though not Macintosh computers). You can find directions for embedding fonts in PowerPoint's *Help* menu.

Keep your font sizes consistent

Keep headlines and body text of the slide in the same font size from slide to slide. Depending on how the presentation will be given and the role that headlines play in your presentation (see discussion that follows about topic headlines versus talking headlines), font sizes for headlines may range from 48 points down to 24 points. Font size for text may go as low as 18 points. Text smaller than that is difficult to read when the presentation is projected.

Position headline flush left and use sentence case

Unless you are consistently using very short headlines, do not center them and do not capitalize every word. Headlines that are flush left and sentence case have a contemporary look and are easy to read.

Always include slide numbers

Page numbers are as important in PowerPoint presentations as they are in a traditional report. They allow your audience a convenient way to refer to a specific slide.

Today's review presentation addresses 4 key items

1. New Product launch schedule

2. Marketing and advertising themes

3. Budget projections

4. Status of distributor contracts

< **Georgia Bold Head**

< Georgia Regular Body

Figure 6.4 Options for coherent font families in slides

Franklin Gothic Demi Head >

Franklin Gothic Book Body >

Today's review presentation addresses 4 key items

1. New Product launch schedule

2. Marketing and advertising themes

3. Budget projections

4. Status of distributor contracts

Today's review presentation addresses 4 key items

1. New Product launch schedule

2. Marketing and advertising themes

3. Budget projections

4. Status of distributor contracts

< **Verdana Bold Head**

< Verdana Regular Body

DESIGNING COHERENT AND READABLE SLIDES

At its best, a PowerPoint slide will quickly capture and focus audience attention. It should not invite the audience to begin reading in detail; an audience who is reading is not listening to the presenter. It also should not confuse the audience by presenting content that does not clearly support the headline or relate to other ideas on the slide.

Below are guidelines and tips to help you create slides that begin communicating their message at first glance and that support their message upon deeper reading.

Write a headline that creates expectations

The headline is the focal point of a slide. Because readers in western cultures generally read from top to bottom and left to right, a headline that begins at the upper left of a slide commands immediate attention. Take advantage of that fact, and write a headline that leads the audience to look for specific content further down on the slide.

The best kind of headline for focusing a reader's attention is a "talking headline"—that is, a short sentence, like a newspaper headline, that makes a key point. Unlike a topic headline that simply announces the topic of a slide, a good talking headline typically makes a claim that the remainder of the slide will support. Notice how, in the examples below, the talking headline focuses your expectations more specifically than the corresponding topic headline.

Topic headline	Talking headline
Percentage of sales by region	Sales are unevenly distributed across regions
Territory market share versus sales potential	Territories with higher market share have higher sales potential
Optimization process	The High Yield Optimization process integrates data about customers, competitors, and products

As Figure **6.5** illustrates, talking headlines will typically require a smaller font size than topic headlines. They also require that you write concisely to encapsulate the key idea.

"Make those slide titles more like newspaper headlines so that your audience won't have to read a dozen lines on the slide and try to decipher your intention."

John Spelich
Vice President
Corporate Communications
Gateway, Inc.

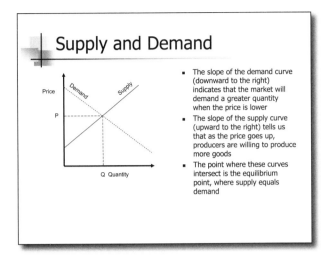

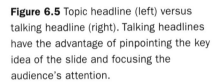

Design the slide content to fulfill headline expectations

This involves determining what material to put on the slide and the best form for that material. In Figure **6.6**, the slide headline asks the audience to look at how SuperTools stakeholders form a complex system and generate many types of data. The slide makes it easy for the audience to find that information by providing a system diagram that highlights stakeholders (ovals), data (document images), and system relationships (arrows). Everything on the slide relates to—and supports—the headline. Nothing is extraneous. Moreover, the information is provided in an ideal form: while the slide could have been designed as a bullet list of stakeholders or a table of stakeholders and data types, the diagram does a particularly good job of showing how all these elements form a complex system.

Figure 6.5 Topic headline (left) versus talking headline (right). Talking headlines have the advantage of pinpointing the key idea of the slide and focusing the audience's attention.

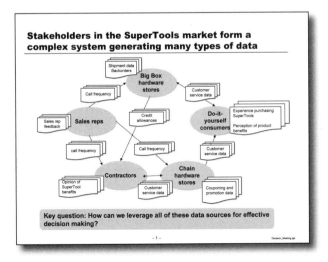

Figure 6.6 Ideally the headline of a slide will raise an expectation and the body of the slide will fulfill that expectation, presenting material in the most effective form: bullet list, table, diagram, photo, illustration, or some combination.

Leave plenty of white space

Viewers need empty space to focus their vision. If a slide is too crowded, your audience may be overwhelmed and see nothing at all. It is better to write a few well-crafted, concise points than to include whole paragraphs on a slide. If necessary, divide an idea between two slides and make each easy to read.

Follow best practices in design of visual elements

For tables, graphs, illustrations, and photos, follow the advice in Chapters 2 and 4 of this book. Be particularly careful about size; the graphic needs to be clearly visible when the image is projected.

Keep text easy to read

PowerPoint's default mode for text is the bullet point layout. This may be one reason writers overuse bullet points rather than using other means of structuring text. As Figure **6.7** illustrates, bullets are certainly a better choice than dense paragraphs of text, as they help readers see the shape of the material at a glance.

2p11

Market Minders' research methodology

Market Minders uses a systematic and collaborative approach to measure brand awareness of our clients' products. First, we work with our clients to establish the purpose of the research. Then we design the study.

Once that is complete, we work with our clients to determine who should respond and how many respondents are necessary. Then, an estimated time line is created. Finally, we develop the survey instrument, execute the survey according to the time line, and meet with our clients to present the results.

Figure 6.7 Compared to paragraphs, bullets allow readers to see key ideas at a glance.

Market Minders measures brand awareness through a systematic research process

• Establish a specific goal for the research

• Design research study

• Determine type and number respondents required

• Establish project time line

• Develop survey instrument

• Conduct survey

• Analyze and present results

> To ensure success, we work collaboratively with our clients at each stage of the process.

However, bullets are not appropriate for all text. They work best for lists: items that can be labeled as members of one category, such as

• reasons	• problems
• steps	• solutions
• examples	• proofs
• respondents	• results
• options	• implications
• patterns	• conclusions

To make the bullets easy to read, be sure they are both logically and grammatically parallel. In other words, all the items should be the same kind of thing and phrased the same kind of way. Figure **6.8** illustrates a before and after version of a slide that has been revised for parallelism.

If your text is not a real list, consider whether you can put it in text boxes, auto shapes, or a diagram that shows the relationship among ideas.

We have studied four potential coating systems for our new lenses

- Polylight two-stage CC coating (the newest Polylight coating)
- Polylight two-stage BB coating (which we use on our current lenses)
- Two single-stage coating systems from different manufacturers
  - Kefvue
  - Reflezene
- We have collected single lot data for the BB and CC coatings and multiple lot data for the single-stage systems.

We have studied four potential coating systems for our new lenses

Two-stage coating systems
- Polylight two stage BB coating (which we use on our current lenses)
- Polylight two stage CC coating (the newest Polylight coating)

Single-stage coating systems
- Kefvue
- Reflezene

We have collected single lot data for the two-stage systems and multiple lot data for the single-stage systems.

Figure 6.8 The headline of the slide above leads a reader to expect that the four bullet points on the slide will list four coating systems. In fact, though, the third bullet contains two systems, and the fourth bullet is an additional comment about the data in the study. The structure of the text serves only to confuse the reader.

The revised slide contains three important revisions: (1) The four bullets correspond to the four coating systems. (2) The coating systems are subcategorized to reflect important groupings. (3) The comment on data is removed from the bullet list and placed in a text box.

SIGNALING THE PRESENTATION FLOW

All presentations benefit from the use of visual techniques that help readers see the overall structure of the presentation and the flow from slide to slide.

Three key design elements of a PowerPoint presentation provide the visual cues your audience needs to grasp the coherence of your presentation.

- Agenda/divider slides that signal the larger sections of your presentations
- Road signs—small textual elements, typically in the upper right hand corner of each slide—that signal where you are in the presentation
- Headlines that signal a logical flow

Agenda/divider slides

In all but the shortest presentations, an introductory agenda or table of contents is crucial to help your audience visualize what territory the presentation will cover and how the parts fit together. In a good agenda slide, the logic of the presentation should be clear at a glance.

An agenda slide, however, is not always sufficient to keep the audience on track throughout the presentation. When you move from one agenda item to the next, you can reinforce the audience's sense of structure by signaling the transition visually with a divider slide that echoes the agenda.

There are a number of ways to display this visual signal. For example, in a black and white presentation, you can place an autoshape box around the agenda item to signal the topic you are addressing next. For a projected presentation on a dark background, you can highlight that agenda item by keeping its text in a high contrast font color, while having the other agenda items rendered in a color that is still distinguishable, yet blends more into the background. Figure **6.9** illustrates this kind of textual approach for an agenda/divider system. It is also possible to create a more graphical agenda slide. Figure **6.10** illustrates an agenda based on the time line for a research process.

"Why have I taken it upon myself to master PowerPoint? When you are dealing with a multinational organization such as 3M, you had better learn to use the tools that are readily available on your desktop."

Dale Bohnert
Public Relations &
Corporate Communications
3M Corporation

Figure 6.9 A system of agenda and divider slides helps readers visualize the structure of a presentation and helps ease the transition from one topic to the next.

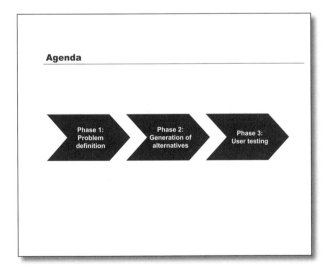

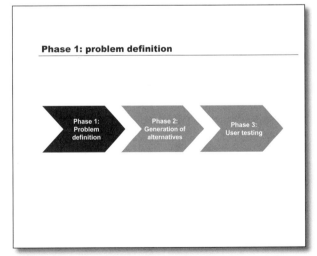

Figure 6.10 Agenda and transition slides can be presented graphically rather than in bullet points.

Road signs

If an agenda slide functions as a road map to signal where a presentation is going and what territory it will cover, then "road signs" on each slide signal where the presentation is right now. Road signs place the name of the agenda item typically in the upper right corner of the slide, as illustrated in Figure **6.11**. If the agenda has presented the structure of the presentation graphically, those graphical symbols can be used for a road sign.

Figure 6.11 A road sign in the upper right corner of the slide provides a visual signal about the position of the slide within the presentation structure.

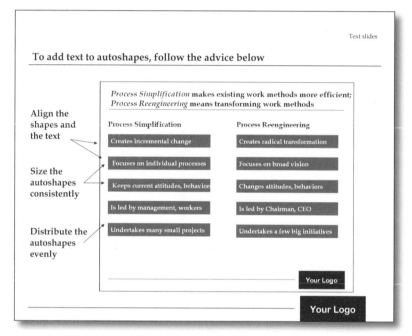

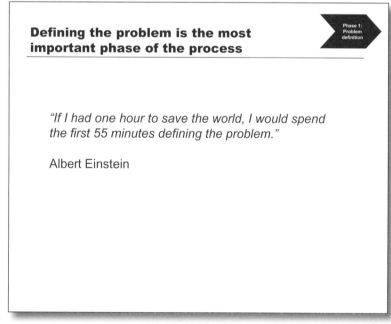

Headlines that signal a logical flow

Slide headlines not only serve to introduce individual slides, they also create flow from slide to slide.

Topic headlines create flow when their logical structure and connection are obvious to the audience. The following headlines, for example, come from a presentation on the evolution of computer games:

- Pre-History: The Arcade
- 1960s–Early 1970s: First Computer Games
- 1970s: First Commercial Attempts

The headlines reflect the chronological structure of the presentation and help keep the audience on track.

Talking headlines create flow when they tell a story. Figure **6.12** shows a series of slides from a presentation about PowerPoint. You can read each headline, in sequence, to follow the story of the presentation.

Figure 6.12 Talking headlines work, across slides, to tell a story.

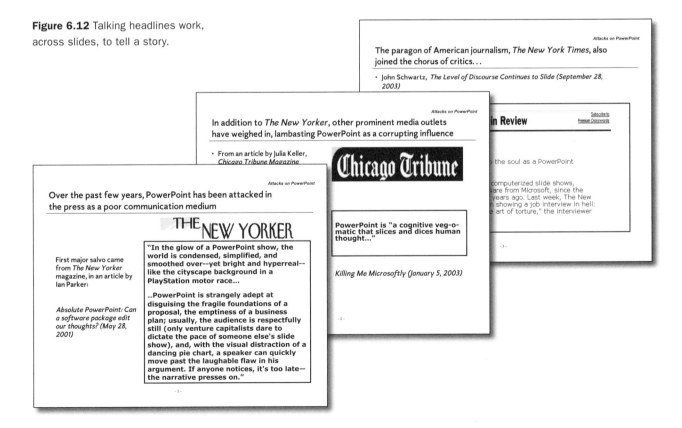

FINAL ADVICE FOR COMMUNICATING IN POWERPOINT

PowerPoint is a powerful visual medium for conveying business messages. To get the most from the medium, we recommend that you consider your presentation document to be a series of canvases on which you can paint pictures that, together, tell a story.

Achieving this goal is challenging

The first challenge is to develop an effective template that creates coherence in your presentation and allows you to paint these pictures well. If you have no corporate standards for your PowerPoint presentations, consider engaging a graphic designer to help you create those standards, following the principles in this chapter. (See Chapter 7, *Selecting a Graphic Designer.*) If you do have corporate design standards, follow the principles we have established here as completely as possible within the restrictions of your organization's requirements. The second challenge is to map out the story, creating headlines for each slide that signal your flow. And the final challenge is to paint the pictures on each canvas well—that is, design slides that capture audience attention, focus on your key ideas, and support what you plan to say.

The final product may not be a work of art, but it will be a work that communicates effectively.

CHAPTER 7 | **SELECTING A GRAPHIC DESIGNER**

In day-to-day work, you are likely to create your own documents, presentations, tables, and graphs with the standard office software. But there may be instances when it is desirable—even essential—to hire a graphic designer.

Large corporations, of course, have the resources to hire designers to help with key projects, such as corporate brochures, annual reports, and other publications. But even start-up and small businesses, with just a few employees, should consider devoting some of their capital to hiring a graphic designer for important visual communications: logos, business stationery, business cards, websites—even templates for reports and PowerPoint presentations. A skilled graphic designer can help you create a polished professional image that may be impossible to achieve on your own. These core designs become the graphic foundation upon which you can create documents and presentations according to the principles in this book.

Why use a graphic designer?

Graphic designers add substantial value in three areas:

Visual identity—Generally, visual identity consists of a number of basic elements that you use to define your business identity. These include your organization's use of colors, typefaces, associated images—and, often, a business logo. All your documents, presentations, and electronic communications will rely on these visual elements. A visual identity should also have a set of written rules that govern how the elements are applied—for example, where a logo is placed on stationery and PowerPoint presentations.[1]

Websites—Because websites are so simple and inexpensive to set up, you may be tempted to design one by yourself. It is better, though, to use a design firm, often a website specialist, to help ensure that your online presentation looks professional and is consistent with your firm's visual identity. Also consider how your website will be maintained and updated in the future. Unlike on printed documents, the content on websites is *constantly* changing.

[1] Mollerup, P. *Marks of Excellence: The history and taxonomy of trademarks.* ©1997 by Phaidon Press.

Marketing communications to customers and prospects—These include product sheets, brochures, poster displays, and other leave-behind selling tools. Even if you plan to distribute only electronic copies (such as Adobe PDFs), a graphic designer can help you create great looking yet functional marketing pieces.

Large firm? small? or freelancer?

Selecting a graphic designer is just like selecting any other professional service provider, such as a lawyer or an architect. You have three dimensions to consider: price, quality, and service. These dimensions are not mutually exclusive. You may get excellent service and high quality at a reasonable price if you choose carefully. However, as with all business decisions, choosing a large design firm, a smaller firm, or an independent freelancer requires balancing a series of trade-offs.

Large, well-established graphic design firms are generally more expensive than smaller firms or individual freelancers. Such large firms may be appropriate if you have complex projects, such as an extensive marketing campaign with multiple materials or an annual report for a publicly traded company. In addition to graphic design capabilities, larger firms can also offer project management services, particularly managing printers, photographers, illustrators, and mailing houses. They may also offer a wide variety of services in non-print media such as radio and TV to help you create an integrated business and marketing presence. Finally, a large design firm that has been around for years provides a sense of stability along with its more extensive capabilities, staff, and resources. A large firm may be especially appropriate if you envision long-term graphic design needs where continuity is important.

Although smaller firms and freelance designers may have fewer resources than a large organization, they may be the better choice if you are looking for personalized service on smaller projects or if your project falls into just one specific category such as website design, print, or multimedia. Many talented designers have chosen the independence of an individual practice over working at a larger more traditionally structured design firm. With today's design software packages, which cost only a few hundred dollars, small firms and

---

A good place to begin your search

"AIGA, the professional association for design, is committed to furthering excellence in design as a broadly-defined discipline, strategic tool for business and cultural force. AIGA is the oldest and largest membership association for professionals engaged in the discipline, practice and culture of designing. AIGA represents more than 16,000 designers."

Source: http://www.aiga.org/

independent freelancers can set up a graphic design practice with only a high-powered computer and a broadband Internet connection. If they need more resources to execute components of your project, small firms and independent designers typically have relationships with a range of established outside vendors.

Defining the scope of your project(s)

In addition to weighing the trade-off between a large firm, small firm, or independent freelancer, you need to establish a well-defined scope and goal for your project. This information will not only help you identify the design capabilities you require; it will also give essential guidance to your designer.

For example, suppose you want to develop a website for your business. What do you want that site to accomplish? Is it going to be simply a marketing presence on the Internet? Are you going to offer products for sale through the website? Do you simply need a designer to create a site in HTML, or will you need sophisticated programming expertise (e.g., ColdFusion, JavaScript, CGI, PHP, and DHTML)?

If you plan to develop a series of marketing pieces for a new service you are offering, are you going to produce a separate marketing piece for each customer segment? One copy for all customer segments? Are you going to create printed copies? Just PDFs to distribute electronically? Both?

A key part of defining the scope of your project is defining what success looks like. Find and analyze what other businesses have done with similar kinds of projects. Developing a website? Look carefully at the websites of organizations that are in a business similar to yours. What components of their websites do you find appealing? What design elements do you like? What do you dislike? Specificity is critical: the more specific you can be about what you want to accomplish, the better the guidance you can give to the designer you hire.

Interviewing Designers

Before you begin interviewing designers, ask to see representative samples from their portfolio—ideally samples that are similar to the project on which you are working. You should also send the designer

"Designers and business people need to work closely together because the design has to support the message. The best designers I've worked with take the time to understand *what* you are trying to communicate and then deliver a design that enhances that message."

Patty Blackburn
Senior Vice President
Corporate Communications
Bank of America Corporation

information about your business, such as materials you have already produced, including business and marketing plans. Give the designer a sense of your business objectives, your business mission, and your business vision. The more a designer knows about your business before you sit down to discuss the project, the better.

When you sit down with a designer, consider asking the following questions:

Where did you receive your graphic design education?
Graphic design requires the mastery of key principles that are best learned in a formal academic setting, though designers with years of experience may have mastered these principles on the job. Many top graphic design programs are accredited by the National Association of Schools of Art and Design, 11250 Roger Bacon Dr., Suite 21, Reston, VA 20190-5248. http://nasad.arts-accredit.org

What is the history of your firm?
Learn as much as you can about the development and growth of the company, especially if you have chosen a smaller graphic design firm. How long have they been in business? How has their expertise changed over time? What is the scale of the projects they can take on? Are they at the leading edge technologically?

Have you worked for a business like mine before? And have you done similar projects?
Designers with experience in your business field or marketplace will have the advantage of being familiar with many of your key business concepts. Similar project experience should allow designers to provide you with more accurate cost and time estimates.

Pick a couple of samples in your portfolio and explain the problem you were asked to solve. What was the solution and how did you arrive at it?
A good designer should be able to show you how he or she thinks. Does the designer offer cookie-cutter solutions to all problems, or are the solutions targeted to customer and user needs?

How have your designs helped your clients increase business or achieve greater visibility?

Good design is not just about aesthetics, but also about meeting specific business goals. The designer you select should give you evidence that he or she understands an organization's needs and can design accordingly.

How many design alternatives will you offer me?

Most designers present at least a few alternative designs to their clients; three alternatives are typical. You should certainly expect more than just one.

How do you price your services?

Most designers price on a per project basis. Design fees are usually priced separately from the cost of illustrations, photographs, and printing. In fact, designers often mark up the price of printing, but they should do so only if they manage the printing process, which includes being on site at the printer as the job is run.

Finally, all proposals should be in writing.

Selecting a website designer

Website design has now become a specialized field requiring not just traditional graphic design skills but programming expertise as well. If you are embarking on the creation of a website, it is a good practice to have your organization's visual identity already completed, so your web designer can make the site consistent with your overall identity.

Below are some tips for evaluating a web design firm:

Start at the firm's own website. It should represent the best work the firm can do. The website should link to samples of the firm's work; evaluate those to see if they demonstrate solutions you want to see.

Identify whether the designer is capable of providing the services you need. Is the individual or firm you have hired capable of developing the back-end functions of your website, such as a database and e-commerce capability? Or are they capable only of designing the look of your site?

Learn how the firm tests a site. Websites are tools that are designed to be used. As such, you need to ensure during the process of website creation that your site undergoes user testing. Are all the links working properly? Is the navigation of your site clear and transparent so that users can move from one page to another without getting lost? If you have an e-commerce application, can users execute a transaction without becoming confused or bogged down?

A final thought

In today's business world—crowded as it is with a huge number of images, logos, and brand identities—a powerful visual presentation will make you stand out. While the principles in this book will take you a long way toward becoming an excellent visual communicator on a daily basis, a skilled graphic designer does have special expertise. He or she will know how to manipulate colors, fonts, and images to create the best impression for a business—and to communicate the messages you want your audience to see.

Great graphic design combines art, technology, and business. Done well, the final results can have a value that goes well beyond the initial investment.

ANNOTATED BIBLIOGRAPHY

In this select bibliography, we have compiled a list of books and articles that we believe are important reading for the business manager who wants to have broad exposure to experts in the field of visual communication.

For example, any business person or scientist who creates tables and graphs should know about William S. Cleveland, John Tukey, and Edward R. Tufte. Those who aspire to senior management positions, where giving presentations is a key part of the job, should be aware of the books by Gene Zelazny—required reading for any strategic planner. And managers who have responsibility for choosing graphic designers, or managing print and online projects where graphic design is critical, should be familiar with key books that address issues of typography and color.

As such, this bibliography leans toward the practical, rather than the academic, and is divided into four sections: Information Display, PowerPoint, Typography, and Color.

INFORMATION DISPLAY: GRAPHS, TABLES

Cleveland, William S. *The Elements of Graphing Data*. Summit, NJ: Hobart Press, 1994.

Cleveland, William S. *Visualizing Data*. Summit, NJ: Hobart Press, 1984, revised edition 1993.

> Cleveland, a statistician and researcher at Bell Laboratories in New Jersey, is one of the pioneers in graph creation. In his books and essays, he systematically addresses methods and principles of graphing and information design. Both of these books are aimed at scientists and technologists but provide useful guidance for the business manager as well. *The Elements of Graphing Data* addresses principles for selecting graphs and methods for designing them, informed by insights about how people perceive information displays; *Visualizing Data* is an extended treatment on graphical methods.

Craig, Malcolm. *Thinking Visually: Business Applications of 14 Core Diagrams*. London SE1 7NX: Continuum, 2000.

> Provides an overview of 14 core business diagrams (such as systems maps, tree diagrams, fishbone diagrams, and flow diagrams), their business application, purpose, and usage conventions.

Few, Stephen. *Show Me the Numbers: Designing Tables and Graphs to Enlighten*. Oakland, CA: Analytics Press, 2004.

> Presents best practices for creating easy-to-understand business graphs and tables. All graphs and tables in the book were created with Microsoft Excel, in part to demonstrate that good design can be achieved using this familiar software tool.

Hargis, Gretchen. *Developing Quality Technical Information*, Upper Saddle River, NJ: Prentice Hall, 1998, 2004.

> Focuses on designing technical documents that are easy to use, are easy to understand, and make information easy to retrieve. It includes an excellent chapter on visual effectiveness.

Harris, Robert L. *Information Graphics: A Comprehensive Illustrated Reference: Visual Tools for Analyzing, Managing, and Communicating*. New York, NY: Oxford University Press, 2000.

> Nearly 500 pages providing some 4,000 illustrations of virtually every kind of graph, chart, and diagram imaginable. Organized alphabetically in an encyclopedia-like format.

Jones, Gerald Everett. *How to Lie with Charts*. Lincoln, NE: iUniverse, Inc., 1995, 2000.

> Shows how graphs can be used to distort information—and how knowing the "tricks" can help you create more effective and truthful presentations.

Kosslyn, Stephen M. *Elements of Graph Design*. New York, NY: W. H. Freeman & Company, 1993.

> Covers the gamut of chart types with practical advice on how to make some key design decisions. Structured in a "Do" versus "Don't" format.

Kostelnick, Charles and David D. Roberts. *Designing Visual Language.* Needham Heights, MA: Allyn and Bacon, 1998.

> Approaches visual design from a rhetorical perspective, arguing that your choice of visual display, and how you design that display, depends on what your purpose is, who your audience is, and how they will use your display.

McMurrey, David A. *Power Tools for Technical Communication.* Ft. Worth, TX: Harcourt College Publishers, 2002.

> A thorough text on all forms of technical communication. See Chapters 10 and 11 for tables and graphics, including a hands-on discussion of how to create them.

Miller, Jane E. *The Chicago Guide to Writing about Numbers.* Chicago, IL: The University of Chicago Press, 2004.

> A book that addresses the presentation of numerical information, including how to organize and present graphs and tables.

Nicol, Adelaide A. M. and Penny M. Pexman. *Displaying Your Findings: A Practical Guide for Creating Tables.* Washington, DC: American Psychological Association, 2003.

> A book aimed specifically at providing guidelines for data displays in psychology studies, though many principles are applicable in business information displays as well.

Schriver, Karen A. *Dynamics in Document Design.* New York, NY: Wiley Computer Publishing, 1997.

> Aimed primarily at graphic designers, this book has a fascinating historical summary of document design. The book takes a psychological and cognitive approach to analyzing how readers view and comprehend documents.

Tufte, Edward R. *The Visual Display of Quantitative Information.* Chesire, CT: Graphics Press, 1983.

Tufte, Edward R. *Envisioning Information.* Chesire, CT: Graphics Press, 1990.

Tufte, Edward R. *Visual Explanations: Images and Quantities, Evidence and Narrative.* Chesire, CT: Graphics Press, 1997.

> Tufte's now-classic books on information design, including his famous discussion of the space shuttle *Challenger* disaster. Memorable words and phrases from these books include "chartjunk" and "adjacent in space, not stacked in time."

Tukey, John. *The Collected Works of John Tukey: Volume V Graphics: 1965-1985.* Cleveland, William S., ed. Pacific Grove, CA: Wadsworth & Brooks/Cole, 1988.

> This book gathers up the essays on graphing of John Tukey, perhaps the 20th century's leading expert on mathematical statistics and the discipline of "exploratory data analysis." Many of these essays are intensely mathematical, yet they offer useful insights on displaying information optimally.

Wainer, Howard. *Graphic Discovery.* Princeton, NJ: Princeton University Press, 2005.

> A book of essays that is part prescription for good design; part history of past, current, and future methods for the visual communication of information; and part graphical exploration of topical subjects such as Supreme Court decisions.

Walkenbach, John. *Excel Charts.* Indianapolis, IN: Wiley Publishing, Inc., 2003.

> A thorough book on creating charts/graphs in Microsoft Excel with a companion CD ROM providing Excel files with actual chart examples. Covers many key software usage issues.

Wurman, Richard Saul, ed. *Information Architects*, New York, NY: Watson-Guptill Publications, 1997.

> A collection of 20 essays, with examples of how information can be communicated clearly using visual elements.

Zelazny, Gene. *Say It with Charts: The Executive's Guide to Visual Communication.* New York, NY: McGraw-Hill, 2001.

Zelazny, Gene. *Say It with Presentations: How to Design and Deliver Successful Presentations.* New York, NY: McGraw-Hill, 2000.

> *Say It with Charts* was a seminal book on using charts and graphs in business. Zelazny refined and implemented his ideas while working as the in-house communication expert for the consulting firm McKinsey & Company. *Say It with Presentations* extends those ideas into the realm of slide presentations.

POWERPOINT

Atkinson, Cliff. *Beyond Bullet Points: Using Microsoft PowerPoint to Create Presentations that Inform, Motivate, and Inspire.* Redmond, WA: Microsoft Press, 2005.

> This book argues that you should use classic storytelling principles when you create PowerPoint presentations.

Shwom, Barbara and Karl P. Keller. *"The Great Man Has Spoken. Now What Do I Do?" A Response to Edward R. Tufte's "The Cognitive Style of PowerPoint."* Oct. 2003 <http://communipartners.com/documents/ComInsV1._000.pdf>.

> Written by two of the authors of this book, this article is a detailed response to Tufte's assault on PowerPoint. The article provides examples of well-designed PowerPoint slides as well as revisions of specific slides that Tufte criticized.

Tufte, Edward R. *The Cognitive Style of PowerPoint.* Chesire, CT: Graphics Press, 2003.

> This pamphlet is a polemic against PowerPoint, arguing that the program lacks the graphical resolution necessary to convey a rich stream of information to an audience.

TYPOGRAPHY

Beaumont, Michael. *Type: Design, Color, Character, Use*. Cincinnati, OH: North Light Books, 1987.

> Written with the typographer/designer in mind, this book offers useful explanations of typography for the nonexpert. It also offers a range of interesting professional examples.

Carter, Rob, Ben Day, and Philip Meggs. *Typographic Design: Form and Communication*. New York, NY: John Wiley and Sons, 1993.

> A comprehensive overview of designing with type. Includes a survey of the fundamental concepts of typographical design including letterform and legibility factors. Also addresses digital technology.

Craig, James, William Bevington, and Susan E. Meyer, eds. *Designing with Type: A Basic Course in Typography*. New York, NY: Watson-Guptill Publications, 1990.

> Used for generations in beginning level typography classes, the updated fourth edition is still one of the very best introductions to the use of typography to convey a message.

Landa, Robin. *Graphic Design Solutions*. Clifton Park, NY: Thomson/Delmar Learning, 2006.

> An introduction and overview of graphic design as an academic discipline and a cultural force, this richly illustrated book contains chapters that cover typography and color, as well as other design principles. Although the discussion of typography is not as thorough as in other suggested books, this book's entire contents may prove useful to nondesign professionals who manage design at any level.

Lupton, Ellen. *Thinking with Type: A Critical Guide for Designers, Writers, Editors, and Students.* New York, NY: Princeton Architectural Press, 2006.

> This book serves as an excellent companion piece to *Designing with Type.* Lupton's book is filled with illuminating example illustrations and includes "Type Crimes," frequently occurring errors in the use of type.

Rabinowitz, Tova. *Exploring Typography: An In-Depth Guide to the Art & Techniques of Designing with Type.* Clifton Park, NY: Thomson/Delmar Learning, 2006.

> A thorough introduction and examination of the history and contemporary practice of typography. This book can be used for either a "deep dive" into the intricacies of typography or as a reference source for better understanding the design of effective layouts, using grids, and understanding typographic terminology.

Spiekermann, Erik and E. M. Ginger. *Stop Stealing Sheep & Find Out How Type Works.* Minneapolis, MN: Sagebrush, 2002.

> As its title suggests, a lively book on the use of type. Includes a discussion of the history and mechanics of type, as well as discussions of how to recognize and choose typefaces and how to use space and layout to enhance communication.

Wolfe, Gregory. *Type Recipes: Quick Solutions to Designing with Type.* Cincinnati, OH: North Light Books, 1991.

> While meant for the graphic designer, this slim volume can give a business manager a solid overview of how type selection can create a particular mood or emotional response. It focuses on ten type families and provides professional examples showing how type choice was used to create a desired effect.

COLOR

Albers, Josef. *The Interaction of Color.* New Haven, CT: Yale University Press, 1963.

> One of the most influential books on color theory, *The Interaction of Color* was created as a teaching aid by acclaimed artist and Yale professor Josef Albers.

Itten, Johannes. *The Elements of Color.* New York, NY: John Wiley & Sons, Inc., 1970.

> Almost four decades since its original publication, this book remains an important contribution to the study of color.

Linford, Chris. *The Complete Guide to Digital Color: Creative Use of Color in the Digital Arts.* New York, NY: Collins Design, 1998.

> A comprehensive overview of digital color design, including how color is managed and used by industry. Addresses concepts such as color organizing systems, e.g., RGB and CMYK; profile color management; file compression; measuring color gamuts; and the use of color in digital photography.

Sawahata, Lisa. *Color Harmony Workbook: A Workbook and Guide to Creative Color Combinations.* Gloucester, MA: Rockport Publishers, 2001.

> A guide that matches colors and color schemes to specific moods. Contains large, tear-out swatches of each color combination for mixing and matching. Also contains a process color conversion chart that gives the CMYK values for the 106 colors used, making the book useful in a digital environment.

Although Microsoft Word is not a page design program, it does allow users to place graphics precisely by using the "frame" tool. This largely undocumented feature of Word allows a user to do two things that are almost impossible to do in the program just by "inserting" or pasting a picture: (1) keep a picture and its caption grouped together, no matter where you move them in the text and (2) place a picture in the margin of a document, as described in Chapter 2 of this book.

The instructions below explain how to configure your copy of Word so that the "frame" tool is visible and usable; insert graphics and captions within a frame; create linked cross-references; move a framed graphic and its caption to a precise location; and update cross-references when figures and tables have moved to a new position in your document.

TO CONFIGURE YOUR COPY OF WORD

1. Make the **Insert Frame** command available by doing one of the following:

   a. Activate the **Forms** toolbar by going to

   View: Toolbars: Forms

   Note: Be sure that the **Forms** toolbar (Figure **1** below) is visible on your screen

   Figure 1 Forms tool bar

   This is the **Insert Frame** icon you will click to add a frame to your text.

   b. Add the **Insert frames** command to your **Insert** menu by doing the following:

      i. On the **Tools** menu, click **Customize**.

      ii. In the window that opens, click the **Commands** tab.

      iii. In the **Categories** box, click **Insert**.

      iv. In the **Commands** box, highlight **Horizontal Frame**.

v. Left-click on **Horizontal Frame** and drag to your **Insert** menu. When the menu displays a list of commands, point to where you want the **Horizontal Frame** command to appear, and then release the mouse.

2. Ensure that you will be able to see how your graphics are anchored to text by making **Object Anchors** visible. Go to:

Tools: Options: View: Print and Web Layout Options: check **Object Anchors**

TO INSERT A GRAPHIC AND CAPTION

1. Place your graphic in a frame by doing the following:

a. Place your cursor where you would like to insert the graphic; be sure that it is after your first reference to the graphic. (This can be at the end of the paragraph that includes the reference.)

b. Either click the **Insert Frame** icon on the **Forms** tool bar or choose **Insert Frame** from the **Insert** menu (depending on what options you made available at the beginning of this procedure). Your cursor will change to a cross hair.

c. With your mouse, drag the cross hair to draw a frame the approximate size you'd like your graphic to be; release the mouse button.

d. Place your cursor in the frame and either paste the picture or click **Insert: Picture** and browse to the picture on your computer.

2. Add a caption by doing the following:

a. Right click on the graphic.

b. In the dropdown menu, highlight **Caption**. A **Caption** window like that in Figure **2** will appear.

Figure 2 Use the caption box to create an automatically numbered caption.

c. From the **Label** dropdown menu, select whether you are adding a caption to a **Figure** or **Table**.

d. From the **Position** dropdown menu, identify the position for the caption as follows:

    i. For figures, select **Below selected item**.

    ii. For tables, select **Above selected item**.

e. Click **OK**. The caption in the **Caption** box will appear in the frame.

f. If you want additional descriptive content in the caption, click on the caption and type the content.

3. Format the frame by doing the following:

a. Right-click on the frame and highlight **Format Frame**.

b. In the popup window (Figure **3**) select your **Text wrapping** option and check the **Move with text** box. Then click **OK**.

4. If there is a black box around the frame, eliminate it by doing the following:

a. Right click on the frame to select the entire frame

b. In the dropdown menu, highlight **Borders and Shading**. A **Borders and Shading** window will appear.

c. In the **Borders** tab, click on the icon **None** box.

d. Click **OK**.

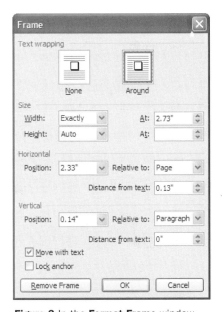

Figure 3 In the **Format Frame** window, you can determine how the frame will be positioned in relation to text.

TO CREATE A LINKED CROSS-REFERENCE

All sentences in your text that refer to specific figures and tables should be electronically linked to the caption of the figure or table. By linking those references to the captions, you will be able to move figures, tables, and text within your document, and Word will automatically re-sequence your caption numbers and all linked references.

1. Place your cursor where you want the linked cross-reference to occur. (For example, in the sentence "As you can see in Figure 3, widgets outsold gizmos by $1,000,000," the words "Figure 3" would be the linked cross-reference.)

2. Go to menu: **Insert: Reference: Cross-reference**. The window in Figure **4** will pop up.

3. In the **Reference type** box, select **Table** or **Figure**.

4. In the **Insert reference to** box, select **Only label and number**.

5. In the **For which caption** box, select the item to which you want to make a cross-reference.

6. Click **Insert**.

7. Go back to your text. You'll see that the words **Figure #** or **Table #** have been inserted.

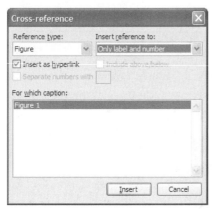

Figure 4 Cross-reference window

TO MOVE A TABLE OR FIGURE TO A DIFFERENT PLACE IN THE DOCUMENT

1. Highlight the entire frame surrounding the figure or table and its caption. (Be sure you highlight the frame and not the figure in the frame.)

2. Right-click and select **Cut**.

3. Move your cursor to the position where you want the figure or table to appear.

4. Paste the frame.

You can also drag and drop by highlighting the frame (and not just the graphic inside the frame) and using your mouse to move the frame.

TO UPDATE CAPTION AND CROSS-REFERENCE NUMBERS

Note: caption and cross-reference numbers should update automatically when you move the frame. However, that doesn't always happen. Thus, you'll need to update your **Fields** as you work.

1. To update a single caption or cross-reference, do the following:

   a. Highlight the caption or cross-reference you want to update.

   b. Right click and select **Update Field** from the drop down menu.

2. To update all the captions and cross-references in a document, do the following:

   a. Put your cursor anywhere in the text of the document.

   b. Press **Control + A** to select the entire document.

   c. Right click and select **Update Field** from the drop down menu.

   d. Double check your document to ensure that all figures, tables, and cross-references are accurately updated.

INDEX